What Are We Afraid Of?

WHAT ARE WE AFRAID OF?

An Assessment
of the "Communist Threat"
in Central America

**A NARMIC-American Friends Service
Committee Study**

by John Lamperti

South End Press   **Boston, MA**

Front cover photo:
Janet Melvin

**Typesetting, design, and layout by the
South End Press Collective.**

Cover by Loie Hayes

Manufactured in the U.S.A.

Library of Congress Cataloging-in-Publication Data
Lamperti, John.
    What are we afraid of?
        Includes index
            1. Central America--Politics and government--1979-
    2. United States--Foreign relations--Central America.
    3. Central America--Foreign relations--United States.
    4. Communism--Central America--History--20th century.
    5. Soviet Union--Foreign relations--Central America.
    6. Central America--Foreign relations--Soviet Union.
    I. National Action/Research on the Military-Industrial
    Complex. II. Title.
    F1439.5.L35 1988   972.8'053   88-6690
    ISBN 0-89608-339-x
    ISBN 0-89608-338-1 (pbk.)
    South End Press, 116 St. Botolph Street, Boston, MA 02115
    98 97 96 95 94 93 92 91 90 89 88   1 2 3 4 5 6 7 8 9 10

John Lamperti lives in Vermont and teaches mathematics and statistics at Dartmouth College in Hanover, New Hampshire. He also works with the peace program of the American Friends Service Committee in New England, and has collaborated several times with AFSC's NARMIC project to produce resources on nuclear power and nuclear weapons. Dr. Lamperti has published two books of mathematics as well as numerous articles both on mathematics and on social issues, and has visited Central America three times since 1985.

When I gave food to the poor, they called me a saint. When I asked why the poor were hungry, they called me a communist.

—**Dom Helder Camara**
Brazilian Bishop,
Nobel Peace Prize nominee

The world is divided into two groups of people: the Christian anti-Communists, and the others.

—**John Foster Dulles**
Secretary of State, 1952-1959

TABLE OF CONTENTS

Acknowledgements

The staff of NARMIC, especially Eva Gold, Tom Conrad and David Goodman, decided in 1985 to encourage a non-specialist to undertake the study which led to this book. I had worked with NARMIC before, but always on issues of nuclear weapons and power; I am grateful that Eva, Tom and David believed I could contribute something useful in a very different area.

I am also indebted to a number of people, both within the AFSC and outside it, who contributed their expertise and time at some stage of the project. Eva Gold has been involved in every phase of the research and writing as advisor and critic. Holly Sklar offered important early help with content and editing. John Sullivan served as editor for NARMIC and worked with me over a period of several months to incorporate disparate advice into an improved final draft. Others who read some or all of the manuscript and offered valuable suggestions include Tom Conrad, Richard Erstadt, William LeoGrande, Mary Morrell, Kenneth Sharpe, Joe Volk and Warren Witte. I also thank David Mac-Michael for the long and (for me) fascinating interview here excerpted in chapter 4, and Janet Melvin for her photo which appears on the cover. Finally, I am grateful to many people on whose writings and knowledge I have relied, even when I do not agree with all their conclusions. Ultimately, all these efforts to find and tell the truth about Central America will help in reforming one of the most misguided and destructive sectors of U.S. foreign policy.

NARMIC/AFSC Statement

The American Friends Service Committee (AFSC) is a nonprofit Quaker-based organization composed of individuals who care about peace and justice. In 1947 it shared a Nobel Peace prize for its work assisting victims of war through provision of humanitarian service.

NARMIC, the research and resource unit of AFSC's Peace Education Division, brings information about the military industrial complex and about U.S. military policy and practices to public attention. AFSC believes that knowing the facts of U.S. militarization will both inform and activate citizens to challenge the encroachments of militarism on U.S. relations with foreign nations, on our democratic institutions, and on the morals and values which the majority of Americans feel U.S. policy should reflect.

In the context of this overall effort NARMIC has produced *What are We Afraid Of? An Assessment of the "Communist Threat" in Central America*. We hope that this level-headed look at the myths and imagined dangers of a communist threat will help to unravel the disinformation campaign systematically employed by our government. Without such reappraisals of the issues which drive U.S. military intervention in Central America, it will be impossible to embark on an alternative which could bring peace and development to the area.

We are grateful to John Lamperti for the contribution of his time and considerable abilities to this project.

—**Joe Volk**
Secretary for Peace Education
American Friends Service Committee
Philadelphia, PA

Preface

The United States is deeply involved in the wars wracking Central America. Washington describes its military role in the region as "low intensity," and so far only a handful of North Americans have died there. But in Nicaragua and El Salvador, where the U.S. government is trying to roll back one revolution and prevent another from gaining power, the picture looks very different. By the end of 1986, for example, the U.S.-sponsored contra war had cost Nicaragua some 16,000 men, women and children killed. These people represent nearly twice as large a fraction of their country's population (roughly three million) as did the 405,000 U.S. dead in World War II. Tens of thousands more Nicaraguans have been wounded or kidnapped, while over 200,000 others have been displaced from their homes by the war. For all this, "low intensity" is a deceptive euphemism.

The U.S. government offers a variety of explanations for its actions, which it claims are both morally right and necessary to satisfy vital national interests. The moral justifications given are often in sharp conflict with actual U.S. policy, and it is hard to believe that moral considerations play any serious role in decision-making. For example, the administration rationalizes its campaign against Nicaragua in part by accusing the Nicaraguan government of serious abuses of human rights. Even if these accusations were all true, however, they would not explain U.S. actions. During the 1970s and 1980s, government forces in neighboring Guatemala murdered and abused the Guatemalan people on a scale that dwarfs the worst allegations, true or untrue, ever made against the Sandinistas—yet the United States did not send arms to the Guatemalan opposition or undertake strong measures to end the killing. (The Carter administration in 1978 halted new aid to the Guatemalan military, which until then had been trained and equipped by the United States, and protested Guatemala's atrocious human rights violations. The terror continued, but the Reagan administration nevertheless moved to restore warmer relations, including renewal of military sales and aid.) The U.S. government consistently ignores or denies atrocities by the forces it backs, the contras in Nicaragua and the military in El Salvador, although many such crimes have been amply documented by independent observers. The claimed U.S. concern about democracy and human rights in Central America is highly selective and applies only to those governments or guerrilla forces which the United States opposes. Genuine concern for the human rights of all concerned plays no serious role in shaping policy.

That leaves perceived national interests as the basis for policy-making. How do U.S. leaders define those interests? The answer is clear from a multitude of speeches, articles and pamphlets, as well as from actual U.S. actions: they believe that the fundamental national interest is to achieve or maintain an advantage over their global adversary, the Soviet Union. Washington regards the USSR as involved in or benefiting from virtually all unrest or rebellion in the Third World. It interprets any challenge to the dominant U.S. role in Central America as an actual or potential part of the Soviet threat, and therefore dangerous to our very survival. Similarly every successful effort to cement U.S. control, whatever the nature of the challenge or the means used to defeat it, is considered a victory over, or at least a denial of opportunity to, the Soviet adversary. For this reason above all, the United States has become the supreme defender of the status quo, especially in what it has long regarded as its own "backyard."

What does the United States really have to fear from revolutionary movements in Latin America? Are they the product of internal conditions of oppression, poverty and corruption? Or are they imported from outside by agitators and arms? Are revolutions like those in Central America part of a coordinated communist drive for global dominance? Does revolution necessarily represent a loss to the United States, and do such U.S. "losses" equal Soviet gains? To evaluate these questions it is essential to describe the possible dangers in specific terms. Images of red ink on the map, still used in government publications, are no substitute for real thought about what a revolution might mean.

Does the Salvadoran revolution, or the Sandinista government in Nicaragua, present a military threat to the United States? What exactly is that threat? Does Nicaragua menace its neighbors either by military action or by subversion, as the U.S. government often charges? Or is the danger one of ideas—that Nicaragua's example may prove attractive to other oppressed peoples? Does the Soviet Union promote revolution in the hemisphere, and if so how? What about Cuba—is it really a "Soviet proxy" as the Reagan administration alleges, and how does it threaten U.S. security? These are the questions which this short book will address.

It is not easy for U.S. citizens to think realistically about Marxism, revolution, and the Soviet Union; decades of anti-communism have produced powerful emotional reactions which can cloud our vision. This study accordingly starts by examining some of these psychological pitfalls. Chapter 2 then describes briefly the policies of the USSR and of Cuba toward Latin America, and chapters 3 and 4 analyze in more detail the charges and realities concerning Nicaragua and El Salvador. The final chapter takes an overall look at how the United States has responded to these challenges, and offers suggestions for change.

U.S. policy in Central America since 1980 has been based mainly on military force. Has this policy addressed the real problems and dangers in the region, or is it headed in the wrong direction? Must the United States choose between national security and acting humanely? Or might another approach, emphasizing diplomacy instead of war, and democracy instead of repression, better serve U.S. interests and simultaneously be true to this country's ideals? Could the United States behave honorably and decently, and protect its national security at the same time? This work has been written in the conviction that a better policy is indeed possible, in the faith that positive change is coming, and in the hope that it will not be too long delayed.

—John W. Lamperti
Hanover, N.H.
December, 1987

1

Thinking About the Problem

Words like "communist," "Marxist-Leninist" and "Soviet threat" are debate stoppers in the United States. For many they create frightening images of red ink spreading over the map. These fears are deeply felt and have a corresponding political impact; few U.S. leaders dare risk being called soft on communism. "...Most Americans can no longer think when they see or hear the word 'communist,'" says a former Peace Corps volunteer in El Salvador. "All forms of logical analysis disappear."[1]

This study attempts to get beyond the generalized fear of communism and ask specifically what dangers to U.S. security could arise from revolution in Central America. It examines the activities of the Soviet Union, Cuba, Nicaragua and El Salvador's insurgency to see what threats and challenges they actually present. And finally it looks into whether United States policy toward the region is helping to solve the real problems there—or is making them worse.

Cold War Image-Making

Clear thinking about these issues is not easy. Decades of anti-communism and cold war propaganda have left a residue of prejudice, a sort of mental scar-tissue that interferes with rational analysis and judgement. George Kennan, a former U.S. ambassador to the USSR and the chief intellectual author of the policy of containment, finds "...the

1

view of the Soviet Union that prevails today in large portions of our governmental and journalistic establishments so extreme, so subjective, so far removed from what any sober scrutiny of external reality would reveal, that it is not only ineffective but dangerous as a guide to political action." He continues:

> This endless series of distortions and oversimplifications; this systematic dehumanization of the leadership of another great country; this routine exaggeration of Moscow's military capability and of the supposed iniquity of Soviet intentions;...this reckless application of the double standard to the judgement of Soviet conduct and our own...these are the marks of an intellectual primitivism and naivete unpardonable in a great government.[2]

Soviet expert Stephen F. Cohen has a name for this syndrome; he calls it "Sovietophobia":

> The United States has two Soviet problems. One is the real but manageable Soviet threat to our national security and international interests. The second, and increasingly more serious, problem is Sovietophobia, or exaggerated fear of that Soviet threat. An old American political disease, Sovietophobia endangers democratic values, distorts budgetary priorities and menaces our national security by enhancing the prospect of nuclear war. Its symptoms include militarized thinking about American-Soviet relations, alarmist assertions about Soviet intentions and capabilities and baseless claims that the United States is imperiled by strategic "gaps"....
>
> Clearly there is a discrepancy between American perceptions and Soviet realities.[3]

The U.S. media and government foster this discrepancy. Cohen points out three ways the media mislead us. First, he argues, they "systematically highlight the negative aspects of the Soviet domestic system while obscuring the positive ones."[4] Soviet achievements such as broadly inclusive social services and rising living standards go largely unreported in this country.

A second offense is the pervasive use of language loaded with unexamined value judgements. Cohen reports, for example, that

> The United States has a government, security organizations and allies. The Soviet Union, however, has a regime, secret police and satellites. Our leaders are consummate politicians; theirs are wily, cunning or worse. We give the world information and seek in-

fluence; they disseminate propaganda and disinformation while seeking expansion and domination.[5]

The third problem is the media's "habit of creating a popular perception that the Soviet Union is guilty of every charge made against it." Examples include trying "to seize Persian Gulf oil" through its invasion of Afghanistan, plotting to assassinate the Pope, and waging chemical war with "yellow rain" in Southeast Asia. In each of these cases the final verdict appears to be not guilty. Yet, "It seems that in the minds of most Americans the Soviet Union remains guilty of all of them." As Cohen explains, "The result is increased acceptance of cold war policies."[6]

"Sovietophobia" seriously distorts U.S. thinking about other nations. One result is the common fallacy that any nation or movement influenced by Marxist ideas must be an accomplice of the USSR and follow policies determined in Moscow. "This kind of thinking is apparently impervious to the extensive historical evidence that refutes it," writes Conor Cruise O'Brien, who points out that

> In the 1950s people like Reagan, by exactly this same reasoning, believed that the Chinese Communists, being Marxists, were *ipso facto* tools of Moscow....But the equation "Marxist equals tool of Moscow," far from being called into question after it broke down in China, is still being applied, with the same overbearing confidence, in Central America.[7]

Misleading or false government "information" is a chronic problem, and led during the Vietnam war era to the infamous "credibility gap." Former Senator J. William Fulbright, at first a supporter of the war, later became one of its leading critics. Asked in 1985 what he had learned from the Vietnam experience, he replied, "Not to trust government statements....They fit the facts to fit the policy." Fulbright continued, "We made a great mistake in Vietnam and we are making another one in Central America."[8]

Before, during, and after the Vietnam War, U.S. leaders deceived the public concerning their actions in Latin America: the Eisenhower administration about the 1954 military coup which the CIA organized in Guatemala; President Kennedy about the Bay of Pigs invasion of Cuba—another CIA operation; Lyndon Johnson about intervening in the Dominican Republic in 1965; Richard Nixon about destabilizing the Allende government in Chile. But despite this record, every generation apparently must learn the lesson anew. "More than Nixon, more than

Johnson, more than either of the Roosevelts, Ronald Reagan has the consummate actor's ability to make things appear to be what they are not," writes John Oakes, the former senior editor of the *New York Times*, adding that

> On no issue of importance is he more adept in the art of deception (and, perhaps, self-deception) than in the relationship of the United States to Latin America.[9]

Patterns of Illogic

Consciously or not, cold-war stereotypes are often reinforced by dubious patterns of thinking. One of these is the "zero-sum" fallacy. In the mathematical theory of games, "zero-sum" means that one player's gains or losses are exactly matched by losses or gains of the others, so that overall nothing is added or subtracted. This describes the transfer of money around a poker table, but it certainly does not apply to the competition between the United States and the Soviet Union. To take the extreme case, nuclear war would be a "play of the game" in which both sides lose disastrously! This point must be less obvious than it appears since statements like this one are heard frequently: "The Soviets are strongly opposed to Star Wars (or the MX missile, or...), so it must be a good thing for us." In reality, weapons such as these which further destabilize the nuclear confrontation lower the security of both sides. The arms race is not a zero-sum game, and neither are most other aspects of foreign policy.

It is nearly universal to measure world events with a double standard. Political debate assumes that U.S. good intentions are beyond question, but no such benefit of doubt is given to countries regarded as adversaries. For example, during the 1962 Cuban Missile Crisis, U.S. leaders insisted that there was absolutely no legitimate comparison between the Soviet nuclear missiles being set up in Cuba and the very similar U.S. Jupiter missiles already based in Turkey near to Soviet territory. The Soviet missiles were simply labeled aggressive while the Jupiters were defensive. The distinction was not widely appreciated outside the United States.

The double standard is especially blatant in the case of Central America. A senior U.S. official there once publicly acknowledged it when a visiting delegation asked him why the United States enthusiastically endorsed El Salvador's elections but condemned those in Nicaragua. The official replied that

> The United States is not obliged to apply the same standard of judgement to a country whose government is avowedly hostile to the U.S. as for a country, like El Salvador, where it is not. These people (the Sandinistas) could bring about a situation in Central America which could pose a threat to U.S. security. That allows us to change our yardstick.[10]

This is a prescription for propaganda, not for analysis; to see clearly and judge fairly it is essential to measure all sides with the same yardstick. That is not always easy. One requirement is that actions must be compared with actions; it is meaningless to weigh actions by one side against the presumed (good or bad) intentions of the other.

Ill-defined abstractions are another source of confusion. For example, saying that "Denmark is a democratic country" implies directly that it has an elected, representative government, but it also suggests high levels of literacy and social welfare, police who respect human rights, and armed forces under civilian control. When the U.S. government describes Guatemala or Honduras as "democratic" there is a strong emotional carryover, even though in these countries illiteracy, poverty and malnutrition are the rule and military forces control civilian authorities more than the reverse. The difficulty is that the key concept, democracy, has not been defined. If we take it to mean elections and little more, then Guatemala and Honduras are democratic—but the warm glow which the word may convey is not justified.[11]

The problem of missing or unclear definitions becomes even worse when "communism" enters the picture. U.S. government publications invariably describe Nicaragua's leadership as "Marxist-Leninist," but what that concept means, and why the United States should fear it, are never explained. A Communist member of the Danish Parliament, a Party member in the Soviet Union or the Peoples Republic of China, and a guerrilla in El Salvador (where all revolutionaries are called communists) may have little more in common than the name. But the name itself is highly loaded, and can impede rational discussion. It can also be used intentionally to direct fear and hatred toward any movement for social change. Speaking about Latin America, an anti-communist Argentine, former diplomat Enrique E. Rivarola, described the problem this way:

In the conduct of internal politics, the "communist threat" has frequently served as a pretext for suppressing social reform movements calling for improved living standards, a more just
distribution of wealth, and participation by the masses in the
government of the country. Those who resist any change in the
traditional structure of society have recourse to the simple ex-
pedient of identifying popular protest with communism and the
legitimate demands of the underprivileged classes with Marxist
subversion.[12]

In the United States too, government officials use the label "communist" to vilify perceived enemies both at home and abroad. A
notorious example is the campaign of slander waged against the late
Dr. Martin Luther King Jr., led by former FBI Director J. Edgar Hoover.
At Hoover's orders the FBI carried out extensive spying and harassment
against King and his associates, accusing King of being a tool of communists in an effort to destroy his leadership and damage the civil rights
movement.[13] The slander resurfaced during the debate over legislation
to declare King's birthday a national holiday.

Impact

There is no question that U.S. political discourse and both foreign
and domestic policies have been shaped by fears of communism. For
example, the Reagan administration always portrays the struggles of
Central American peoples as part of the global U.S./Soviet competition.[14] Any social movement which challenges U.S. control is seen as a
gain for the Soviet side. President Reagan and his associates consistently describe the United States—the strongest military power in world
history—as threatened and embattled, beset by treacherous enemies
on its very doorstep.

It is vitally important to find out how much truth this picture contains. Has the Soviet Union deliberately chosen this region as the bat-
tleground for an attack on the United States? What is the evidence? Do
the Sandinistas of Nicaragua or the revolutionaries of El Salvador really threaten "the safety of our homeland" as Mr. Reagan says?[15] Or is it
possible that the president's apocalyptic rhetoric serves as camouflage
for more mundane U.S. interests? The next three chapters will examine
the record.

2

The Russians (and the Cubans) Are Coming—Aren't They?

Let's not delude ourselves. The Soviet Union underlies all the unrest that is going on.

—Ronald Reagan, 1981

There is a Soviet threat, just as there is a U.S. threat. The United States could be virtually obliterated in a few hours if the Soviet Union chose to fire its nuclear arsenal, committing suicide in the process. U.S. military forces have the same life-or-death power over the USSR. Both superpowers hold civilization hostage to nuclear holocaust.

In October 1962 the world experienced the tense "thirteen days" of the Cuban missile crisis, when the Soviet Union secretly began to install nuclear-armed missiles in that Caribbean nation. The United States responded with a partial naval blockade of Cuba and with outraged rhetoric demanding that the "offensive" Soviet missiles be removed. Leaders of both superpowers thought that the crisis might escape their control and lead to war; President John Kennedy later estimated the chances as between one-third and even. Eventually the U.S. government presented the Soviets with an ultimatum, insisting that they must remove their missile bases or the United States would destroy them. Apparently to Kennedy's surprise, Soviet Premier Krushchev agreed to withdraw the Soviet missiles in exchange for lifting the blockade and a public U.S. pledge not to invade Cuba—plus a secret U.S. promise to withdraw its fifteen nuclear missiles from Turkey.[1]

Avoiding such crises in the future must be an overriding objective for U.S. policy. Fortunately, the danger of a replay in the Caribbean or Central America appears remote. The informal no missiles/no invasion bargain of 1962 has so far been kept, although both sides have probed its limits and ambiguities. Today the USSR would have little to gain by basing strategic missiles in Cuba. In 1962 the overwhelming superiority of U.S. nuclear forces must have figured largely in the Soviet decision to seek a quick fix—the Cuban bases—to reduce that imbalance. The fix didn't work, and the Soviet Union embarked on a major nuclear build-up. In the late 1960s rough parity was reached, removing one motive for the Cuban deployment. Moreover, since 1967 most Latin American nations have signed and ratified the Treaty of Tlatelolco, establishing their territories as a zone to remain free of nuclear weapons. Equally important, all five avowed nuclear-weapons powers have signed and ratified Protocol II to this treaty, by which they pledged to respect the nuclear-free status of the region.[2]

It appears highly unlikely that the Soviet Union or Cuba would deliberately take actions which could provoke a U.S. military response against Cuba. As General Wallace Nutting, the former chief of the U.S. Southern Command, observed in 1983,

> if push comes to shove in this region, the outcome is not in doubt. It would be very difficult for the Soviet Union to project the kind of conventional power into the Caribbean Basin that we can't deal with. If we were ever faced with a major confrontation, we would prevail.[3]

But what if mounting tensions in some future crisis should lead to a new U.S. attack on the island? The Soviet leaders would face a harsh dilemma. If they took no strong action, they would risk the destruction of an ally in which the USSR has a major investment of resources and prestige, and the political costs would be great. Assuming General Nutting is right, conventional military power would be inadequate for Cuba's defense. Would the Soviets then take action elsewhere in the world where the United States might be at a disadvantage? Or would using nuclear weapons seem their only choice?

Clearly the Soviet government does not wish to have to choose among these alternatives, and the USSR has been careful not to give Cuba any public guarantee of military support such as membership in the Warsaw Pact. This potential dilemma has certainly been a factor in the Soviet Union's support for Cuba's military buildup. To the extent that Cuba can defend itself, or (even better) can deter attack, Soviet decision-making is greatly simplified.

Can Cuba Threaten the United States?

Cuba's armed forces are bigger and better-equipped than any others in Latin America except those of Brazil, to which the Cuban military is very roughly comparable. The Cuban air force operates some 262 combat aircraft including 196 MiG-21 and 51 MiG-23 fighters, plus 80 transport planes of various types and about 120 helicopters, 42 of them armed. The relatively large army is well equipped with tanks, artillery and anti-aircraft weapons. Some 28,000 troops are stationed abroad, almost all of them in Africa. Finally, Cuba's navy includes three Soviet-built, diesel-powered attack submarines, two frigates, eighty-five patrol and attack boats, plus fifteen minesweepers.[4]

Since the 1961 Bay of Pigs invasion attempt, the Cuban revolution has felt itself to be under threat from the United States. One mission for Cuba's military is to deter attack by ensuring that any U.S. invasion would be a major and costly undertaking. As military analysts Joseph Cirincione and Leslie Hunter describe it,

> The Cuban build-up has largely achieved its defense objectives. A U.S. invasion of the island would now require an estimated 100,000 American troops and the deployment of more carrier battle groups than the United States could afford to commit. The U.S. would undoubtedly sustain heavy casualties in such an operation. This is probably not an option that the United States would be inclined to exercise except in the most dire emergency.[5]

This deterrent value of Cuba's military forces may have been tested in the early days of the Reagan administration. According to *Newsweek* magazine,

> As the men in his [Ronald Reagan's] innermost circle knew, he had had to be dissuaded from the private fantasy that Cuba might be liberated by force of arms; the appraisal of the CIA was that Fidelistas would simply take to the hills again and turn the island into a front-porch Vietnam.[6]

Cuba's military strength does not, however, add up to a serious independent offensive capability, certainly not one which could operate in the face of U.S. opposition. In the Caribbean Basin the United States has deployed over 14,000 troops at a complex of U.S. air, sea and naval bases, while thousands more participate annually in military exercises in the region.[7] The area is continually patrolled by four to twenty ships of the U.S. Navy.[8] Puerto Rico, assigned a leadership role in implementation of U.S. Caribbean military policy, is home to Roosevelt Roads Naval Station, the largest U.S. naval base in the hemisphere. The U.S. military has contingency plans to deploy nuclear weapons to Puerto Rico in a possible future crisis, and, according to a study by the Puerto Rican Bar Association, Roosevelt Roads already "is prepared to function as a center for command and control for nuclear weapons, as well as a base from which nuclear weapons could be deployed."[9] The U.S. Southern Command in Panama, which oversees U.S. forces in South and Central America and the Caribbean, was upgraded in 1983 to a post of four-star rank, and Honduras has been turned into a logistical center for operations with the permanent deployment of a joint task force involving over a thousand military personnel while many more troops rotate through on short-term assignments. The Pentagon has expanded military facilities throughout the region—in Panama, Puerto Rico, Guantanamo Bay (Cuba), Key West (Florida), and especially in Honduras where the United States has built or upgraded eleven air bases, as well as radar stations, military roads and other facilities. Almost continuous land, sea and air exercises have practiced rapid deployment of troops, ships and equipment to the area under a variety of possible scenarios for military action. At least 80,000 U.S. troops have trained in Honduras alone since 1983.[10]

A frequently cited cause for concern is a possible Cuban threat to shipping in the Caribbean, and to the Panama Canal. One Reagan administration document states that

> The major shipping lanes crisscrossing the region make it one of our major lifelines to the outside world, and, as a result, an area of crucial importance to the continued prosperity and security of the United States. The defense of the Caribbean, however, is complicated by hostile forces in Cuba and Nicaragua within easy reach of these sea lanes.[11]

The region is indeed important, but are the shipping lanes in any real danger? A September 1985 study by the congressional watchdog, the General Accounting Office, reports that fears about Cuban and

Soviet influence in the Caribbean have been used in justifying both the Grenada invasion and administration requests for increased military aid to Central America. The study finds, however, that "U.S. and Caribbean officials perceive little immediate threat from internal political instability or external intervention despite the current unrest in Central America."[12]

Former Ambassador to Nicaragua Lawrence Pezzullo commented bluntly on these questions in a 1983 interview:

> With the advent of the ICBM and Yankee-class [Soviet] submarines off our coast, how the hell can you talk about strategic interests? And all of that business that the traffic coming through the Caribbean is so vital to our interests—the fact of the matter is you've got Cuba in the Caribbean for the last twenty years. They could have intercepted those lanes any time. You didn't need Nicaragua. You didn't need the airfield in Grenada. This is just hyperbole.[13]

Any Cuban attack on U.S. shipping in the Caribbean or on the Canal would be an act of war; so would a move against Mexican or Venezuelan oil fields, another threat occasionally cited by the administration. Under what conditions could such attacks make sense to the Cuban government? The answer seems to be "none at all." For Cuba to act on its own, or as part of some regional conflict not involving the USSR, would be not only pointless but also suicidal in the face of overwhelming U.S. military superiority.

Is it more credible that Cuba would act against Caribbean "Sea Lanes of Communications" (SLOC) as a Soviet ally? The April 1984 *White House Digest* asserts that Cuba has "the potential for delaying the reinforcement of NATO in time of general war." A general war between the superpowers, however, would in all likelihood not be confined to European soil or conventional battlefields but would involve strategic nuclear weapons. In this case, concern about Cuban attacks on Caribbean shipping or on Mexican oil would be far from the minds of the survivors. In the unlikely event of a non-nuclear world war, the delay in reinforcing NATO which Cuba could cause has been estimated as probably lasting only a few days.[14] It is doubtful that the Cuban government would choose to sacrifice the nation to provide such marginal help to Soviet forces in Europe. Analysts including U.S. Marine Corps Lt. Colonel John Buchanan (ret.) believe that armed neutrality would be Cuba's only hope for survival in the event of such a war, and that the Cuban leaders are well aware of these realities.[15]

The Soviet Union does obtain certain military benefits from its relationship with Cuba, such as a site for electronic intelligence-gathering and landing fields for long-range reconnaissance flights. Soviet naval vessels are routinely sent to the Caribbean for joint exercises with Cuban forces; from 1969 to mid-1986 there were twenty-six such deployments, typically involving four Soviet ships, two of them combatant ships, and lasting about one month.[16] These activities are small-scale compared to the U.S. military presence near Soviet territory. In East Asia and the Pacific alone the United States has over 90,000 troops and maintains nineteen air, seven naval and six ground force bases, not including over 16,000 U.S. troops at eleven large and small naval and air bases in the Philippines. The Seventh Fleet at sea includes seventy-five to eighty ships and some 20,000 crew members; the only overseas-based U.S. aircraft carrier, the *Midway*, is home-ported in Japan along with its escort and support vessels.[17]

The large-scale U.S. military involvement with countries on the USSR's periphery must worry Soviet strategists, just as the Soviet military relationship with Cuba appears threatening to U.S. planners. But although these third-party involvements can be dangerous and destabilizing, they are not the core of the problem. The underlying source of danger is the military competition of the superpowers themselves, which threatens the entire globe with destruction.

Soviet Policy Toward Latin America

Except for Cuba, the nations of Latin America have played only a small role in the foreign policy of the Soviet Union. Just three countries—Mexico, Argentina and Uruguay—have maintained diplomatic contacts with the USSR continuously since 1945. (See Figure 1.) One lengthy Soviet history of the USSR's foreign policy devotes only fourteen out of 1,013 pages to Soviet relations with Latin America, and half of these cover relations with Cuba.[18] U.S. State Department figures indicate that in 1981 under 2 percent (measured by dollar value) of Soviet military agreements with "Less Developed Countries" (LDCs) were with Latin America; for the USSR's Eastern European allies the corresponding figure was under half a percent. (By the State Department's definition, LDCs include all the nations of Latin America and the Caribbean except Cuba.) That same year the USSR had some 16,280 military technicians in LDCs, of whom only 1 percent were in Latin America, along with sixty (3 percent) from Eastern Europe out of its analogous total of 1,925.[19]

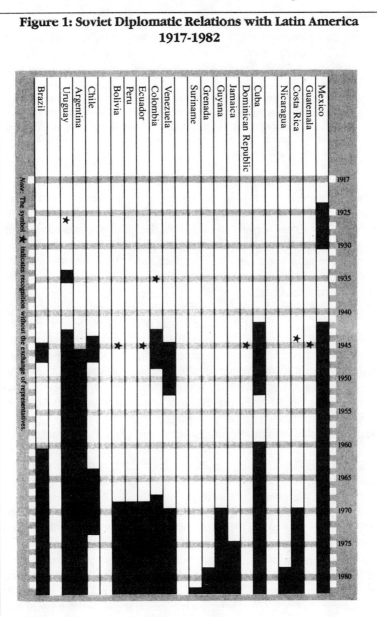

Figure 1: Soviet Diplomatic Relations with Latin America 1917-1982

Source: Blasier, Cole, *The Giant's Rival: The USSR and Latin America.* University of Pittsburgh Press, 1983, p. 17. Reprinted with permission.

The idea that Moscow has been the instigator of discontent and revolutionary movements throughout the hemisphere, often repeated by the U.S. government, doesn't square with historical reality. As summed up by Soviet expert Jonathan Steele,

> Latin America during the Brezhnev era provided a clear pattern of evidence that the Soviet Union puts support for revolution low on its list of priorities....It failed to give material backing to the numerous urban and rural guerrillas operating in most Latin American countries during the two decades.[20]

The Soviet Union's real priority in Latin America has been establishing beneficial diplomatic and economic relations with as many nations in the region as possible. The USSR has pursued this goal with substantial success, especially since the late 1960s. Soviet trade with Latin America grew rapidly during the 1970s, with the value of imports from the region consistently exceeding the value of Soviet exports. Trade between the United States and Eastern Europe also expanded greatly during this period.[21]

The USSR has based its choice of trading partners less on political or ideological sympathies than on the needs of the Soviet state. For example, the Soviet Union's largest Latin trading partner is Argentina, from which it imports large quantities of such agricultural products as grain, meat and wool. A huge impetus to this trade came in 1979 when the United States put an embargo on grain sales to the USSR in response to the invasion of Afghanistan. The U.S. government pressed Argentina to join the embargo, without success. Instead Argentina was eager to take advantage of its new market opportunity, and in one year its sales to the Soviets, already substantial, increased fourfold to well over one billion rubles (more than a billion dollars). This trade doubled again the following year, by which time the USSR was taking about one-third of Argentina's exports.

These were the years when Argentina's military rulers conducted their "dirty war" against all forms of internal opposition. Military and police forces with impunity tortured and murdered thousands of their fellow citizens, while thousands more were kidnapped and made to "disappear." Political parties of the left, including the Communist Party, were outlawed. But the Soviet Union muted its criticism, abstaining from votes on UN resolutions which condemned Argentina for human rights violations. The contrasting case of Chile, where the USSR broke off diplomatic relations after the overthrow and assassination of elected socialist President Salvador Allende in 1973, was exceptional.

Table 1: Pro-Soviet Communist Party Membership in Latin America, 1962, 1973, 1982

	1962	1973	1982
Argentina (PCA)	50,000	70,000	70,000-125,000
Bolivia (PCB)	4,000-5,000	—	500 (1980)
Brazil (PCB)	25,000-40,000	6,000	10,000
Chile (PCCh)	18,000-20,000	120,000	—
Colombia (PCC)	8,000-10,000	10,000	12,000
Costa Rica (PVP)	300	1,000	3,200
Cuba	27,000	120,000	434,143
Dominican Republic (PCD)	—	470	—
Ecuador (PCE)	2,000-3,000	500	1,000 (1979)
El Salvador (PCES)	500	100-150	200
Guadaloupe (CPG)	—	3,000	—
Guatemala (PTG)	1,000-1,100	750	750
Guyana (WPVP)(PPP)	—	100	500 (PPP)
Honduras (PCH)	1,500-2,000	300	1,500
Martinique (CPM)	—	1,000	—
Mexico (PCM)	5,000-6,000	5,000	100,000
Nicaragua (PSN)	200-300	60 (PSN)	1,200
Panama (PCP)	150	500	500-600
Paraguay (PCP)	5,000	3,000-4,000	3,500
Peru (PCP)	5,000-7,000	2,000	3,200
Uruguay (PCU)	3,000	22,000	7,500
Venezuela (PCV)	20,000	3,000-4,000	—

Sources: For 1962, U.S. Department of State, Bureau of Intelligence and Research, *World Strength of the Communist Party Organizations* (Washington, D.C.: U.S. Government Printing Office, 1962); for 1973, ibid. (1973); for 1982, *Yearbook of International Communist Affairs 1982* (Stanford, CA, 1982).
Note: Prepared by Aldo Isuani and Aldo Vacs.
— = not available, unknown.

Tables 1 and 2 show that outside of Cuba, membership in the local Communist Parties and communist participation in legislative bodies is low. Both characteristics suggest that communist political influence on the electorate is not great.

Source: Blasier, *The Giant's Rival,* p. 76. Sources listed above appeared with the original table and are reprinted here for the reader's information. Reprinted with permission.

Table 2: Electoral Strength of Pro-Soviet Communist Parties in Latin America, 1971-1981

	Percentage of Votes	*Seats in the Legislature*
Argentina		2 of 312 (1973)
Bolivia[a]		
Brazil		5 (1981)
Chile	16.90 (1971)	29 of 200 (1970)
Colombia	1.9 (1978)	3 of 311 (1978)
Costa Rica	7.0 (1978)	3 of 57 (1978)
Dominican Republic	—	—
Ecuador	3.2 (1979)	11 of 69 (1979)
El Salvador	—	—
Guadeloupe		7 of 36 (1976)
Guatemala	—	—
Guyana		10 of 43 (1980)
Haiti	—	—
Honduras	—	—
Jamaica	—	—
Martinique	—	3 of 36 (1979)
Mexico	5.4 (1979)	18 of 300 (1979)
Nicaragua	—	—
Panama		1 (1980)
Paraguay	—	—
Peru	5.9 (1978)	6 of 100 (1978)
Uruguay[b]	6.0 (1966)	
Venezuela	9.0 (1978)	22 of 195 (1978)

Sources: Yearbook of International Communist Affairs, 1982 (Stanford, CA, 1982), except for Argentina, ibid., *1974*, p. 227, and *La Prensa* (Buenos Aires) 12 March 1973; Chile, *Yearbook, 1973*, p. 305; Uruguay, *ibid.,* 1972, p. 429.

Note: Table prepared by Aldo Isuani and Aldo Vacs.

[a]In the 1980 elections, communist candidates were absorbed into the Union Democratica Popular.

[b]In the 1971 elections, Communist candidates were absorbed into the Frente Amplio.

—means either that the party did not participate in the election or that it received no recorded votes. A blank space has been left in column 2 when the party participated as part of another group and its own total is unknown.

Source: Blasier, *The Giant's Rival,* p. 77. Sources listed above are reprinted for the reader's information. Reprinted with permission.

In addition to conventional state-to-state relations such as trade and diplomacy, the Soviet Union exerts some influence in most Latin countries through the existence of communist parties whose programs are roughly consistent with Moscow's policy. U.S. leaders frequently portray such parties as foci for subversion and tools of Soviet expansionism, but the reality is different and more complex. Throughout the continent, a great variety of left-wing political parties are actively working for social change, including many which explicitly reject Moscow's leadership. The pro-Soviet parties have generally been moderate in their tactics, and as a rule have rejected armed struggle and worked for change by participation in elections, trade union organizing, publishing magazines and newspapers, and coalition building—in short, by conventional political activities. The most militant activists have sometimes split from these parties in order to form new groups which adopt more aggressive strategies. In a few countries, including Cuba, Nicaragua and El Salvador (since 1979), the pro-Soviet communists have joined as latecomers in armed rebellions which were already far advanced under other leadership. Since the 1930s no conventional, pro-Moscow communist party in Latin America has played an important role in creating armed insurrection.[22]

The orthodox communist parties of Latin America (other than Cuba) are small numerically and have usually attracted little support at the polls when they have been able to participate in elections. (See Tables 1 and 2.) The major exception was Chile in the 1970 elections, when the Chilean Communist Party won twenty-nine seats in the 200-member legislature and thereafter participated in the government as a junior partner of Allende's Socialist Party in the Popular Unity Coalition. Latin America's communist parties are miniscule in comparison with parties in some NATO nations. The largest of these, the communist party of Italy, claims over 1,670,000 members and received 30.5 percent of the vote in 1983 elections.[23]

The Impact of the Cuban Revolution

The Cuban revolution belies any claim that the Soviet Union is behind all revolutionary upheavals. Before the revolution's 1958 victory, the existing Moscow-oriented Cuban communist party (the Partido Socialista Popular, or PSP) was entirely separate from Fidel Castro's 26th of July Movement. The PSP was dedicated to the "peaceful road" of mass organizing, and had in the past collaborated with the Batista regime. At times the PSP directly opposed the tactics of the Fidelistas; in particular, the PSP strongly condemned as "adventurist" the famous 1953 attack on the Moncada barracks. Only a few communists ever joined the guerrilla groups. When the armed forces of the old regime collapsed with unexpected speed, surprising all concerned and forcing dictator Fulgencio Batista to flee Cuba on December 31, 1958, the broad opposition front envisioned by the PSP had not yet been established. As a result, the PSP had not joined the armed combat to any substantial degree or formally allied itself with Fidel Castro's movement. Its contribution to the actual overthrow of Batista was minimal.[24]

The United States recognized the new Cuban government on January 7, 1959, and for a brief period good relations seemed possible. Soviet recognition also came quickly on January 11, but more substantial contacts with the USSR, including the first trade agreement and formal diplomatic relations, were delayed until (respectively) February and May of the following year. By that time United States hostility to the revolution had already hardened, and in March 1960 President Eisenhower authorized the CIA to begin recruiting and training Cuban exiles for sabotage, commando raids and an invasion. Other U.S. anti-Cuba measures included halting purchases of Cuban sugar and maintaining an arms embargo. The USSR then moved to fill many of Cuba's increased needs by purchasing much of the sugar formerly going to the United States, by supplying oil, and by beginning to provide the "necessary aid" to allow Cuba to resist armed intervention. Although U.S. hostility to Cuba and the increasing ties between Cuba and the Soviet Union clearly reinforced each other, the break between Cuba and the United States was originally provoked mostly by U.S. dislike of Cuba's domestic policies and revolutionary rhetoric.[25]

From late in 1960 through early 1962 the Soviet commitment to Cuba's aid and defense increased steadily. Despite Cuba's growing dependence, however, Soviet and Cuban interests and policies often diverged. During the 1962 missile crisis, for example, Cuban leaders were outraged that Washington and Moscow negotiated a settlement without Cuban participation. Cuba refused to accept UN inspection to verify that the missile bases were actually dismantled, and tried unsuccessfully to impose additional conditions as part of the crisis settlement by demanding an end to attacks on Cuba from U.S. territory and the return of the U.S. naval base at Guantanamo Bay to Cuban control. A month later the Cuban government officially expressed its displeasure with the U.S.-Soviet agreement, declaring that "An armed conflict has been avoided, but peace has not been achieved."[26]

The most important area of Soviet/Cuban disagreement was strategy for social change in Latin America. Revolutionary Cuba's early attempts at accommodation with the more progressive Latin American states soon gave way to support for armed revolution as the only real path to social progress. This support frequently conflicted with Soviet policy; it also evoked suspicion of Cuban intentions from a wide spectrum of Latin American governments. At the same time, the United States worked with unrelenting hostility to isolate Cuba diplomatically. As a result both of U.S. pressure and of Cuba's aid to revolutionary movements, the Organization of American States voted to impose sanctions against Cuba in June 1964.

Cuba sometimes found itself at odds with local pro-Soviet communists as well as with the USSR itself. In 1965, for example, the Venezuelan Communist Party (PCV) withdrew from a losing armed struggle against the government. Fidel Castro denounced the party as defeatist, and added that Cuba would support groups engaging in armed revolutionary struggle regardless of whether or not they called themselves communist. Cuban backing was shifted from the PCV to a splinter group of guerrillas, who received some arms aid and a few Cuban volunteers to assist their fight. In 1967 the PCV actually joined the Venezuelan government in denouncing Cuba for outside interference. At the same time, the USSR was trying to reestablish normal relations with Venezuela, an attitude naturally resented by Castro and his guerrilla allies.[27]

While Cuba maintained an ideological commitment to revolution during these years, the policy was not a practical success. For one thing, the resources to provide major assistance were not available. The Soviet Union did not support Cuba's enthusiasm for guerrilla movements, and what Cuba could do on its own was limited; the number of instances of Cuban involvement, and the amounts of material aid given, were modest. The same is true of Cuban training for leftist organizers or guerrillas: Cuba did provide training for some 2,500 men and women during the 1960s, but this was far less than the numbers estimated at the time.[28] The involvement of the United States during the same period was much greater. Between 1950, when U.S. training programs began in earnest, and 1970, 54,270 members of Latin American armed forces received U.S. military training, and from 1961 to 1973 an additional 3,842 security personnel received police training in the United States under the U.S. Public Safety program, while thousands more were trained abroad.[29]

Despite the instances of Cuban support, attempts at guerrilla-style revolution in Latin America during the 1960s were uniformly unsuccessful. By 1967, guerrilla movements in Peru and Argentina had been beaten, and those in Venezuela, Colombia and Guatemala were disorganized and under strong attack. Also in 1967, the Bolivian army (with U.S. help) captured and assassinated Cuba's revolutionary hero Che Guevara; the defeat of Che's guerrilla campaign in Bolivia epitomized the failure of Cuban attempts to assist revolutions abroad.

A major change in Cuba's foreign policy became evident after 1968, and its support for armed revolutionary struggle waned. Soviet pressure, as well as the failure of Cuban-aided guerrilla attempts, undoubtedly contributed to the reversal. In addition, the success of Allende's movement in Chile seemed for a time to show that revolutionary social change could be achieved through peaceful, democratic means. Castro was reportedly outraged when a bloody coup ended Allende's life and Chilean democracy in 1973, and he bitterly blamed the United States for instigating and organizing the coup. But even in this extreme situation, which provoked the Soviet Union to the rare step of breaking diplomatic relations with Chile, Cuban leaders did not consider armed intervention to be a viable response.

Cuba's new attitude gradually succeeded in reassuring neighboring governments. The first to reestablish diplomatic relations with Cuba was Allende's Chile in November 1970, but more conservative states soon followed suit. By the mid-1970s diplomatic relations had been reestablished with over a dozen Latin American nations—plus Mexico which alone had never broken them. The OAS sanctions against Cuba were repealed in 1975. Cuba had ended its hemispheric isolation and become an accepted neighbor to most of its sister nations. The process still continues; in June 1986 Cuba and Brazil restored diplomatic ties.

United States/Cuban Relations Since 1974

In 1972 the Nixon administration began its historic approach to the People's Republic of China, ending years of bitter animosity. This changed attitude toward the world's most populous communist nation, as well as Cuba's newly-moderate foreign policy, made some sort of rapprochement between Cuba and the United States appear logical. The benefits were obvious, and in 1974 secret meetings were held to discuss terms for reestablishing relations. But conflict outside the Western Hemisphere brought the tenuous process to a halt.[30]

In 1975 Cuba and the United States became deeply involved in aiding different sides in the struggle over Angolan independence. Cuba supported the Popular Movement for the Liberation of Angola (MPLA), while the United States, South Africa and China backed two other factions. When a South African armored column invaded Angola in October 1975, joining forces with Jonas Savimbi's National Union for the Total Independence of Angola (UNITA) in a drive north toward the capital Luanda, Cuba promptly dispatched combat troops to the aid of the MPLA. The operation was a Cuban, not a Soviet, initiative, and the first troops were sent to Africa using Cuban ships as transports; later Soviet planes airlifted additional Cuban forces. By March 1976 the MPLA controlled nearly all of newly-independent Angola.

For Cuba the operation seemed a clear success, both militarily and politically; South Africa's invasion gave the Cuban intervention legitimacy. Third World reaction was overwhelmingly positive: Cuba was commended by the Organization of African Unity and by the Movement of Nonaligned Nations, which later chose Cuba to head the group. The action was also popular at home, an occasion for national pride unequalled since the victory at the Bay of Pigs in 1961.

But Cuba's Angolan intervention was not popular in Washington, which interpreted it as a Soviet thrust for power. John Stockwell, head of the CIA's Angola Task Force in 1975-76, described U.S. policy this way:

> Uncomfortable with recent historic events, and frustrated by our humiliation in Vietnam, Kissinger was seeking opportunities to challenge the Soviets. Conspicuously, he had overruled his advisers and refused to seek diplomatic solutions in Angola.[31]

The MPLA/Cuban victory was therefore interpreted as an embarrassing defeat for the United States, and the tentative U.S.-Cuban normalization process was stopped in its tracks.

Cuban involvement in Africa continued to prevent improved relations with the United States, even though the Carter administration revived the U.S./Cuba talks in 1977. Late that year Cuban armed forces helped Ethiopia repel an invasion from Somalia; the Cubans stayed on to provide at least passive support for Ethiopia's 1978 campaign against the attempted secession of Eritrea. Once more the United States found Cuba's activism in Africa unacceptable, and normalization of relations was again halted. Sporadic meetings have been held since that time, but the normalization process has made little progress.

Since 1981 the Reagan administration has pictured Cuba as a major force behind revolution in Central America and the Caribbean.[32] Former Secretary of State Alexander Haig threatened that the United States might "go to the source"—Cuba—to combat revolution. Presumably in response to such threats, Cuba increased its military imports from the USSR. The Cuban government again indicated a desire to improve relations with the United States, but the Reagan administration was not interested; it subsequently imposed new measures against Cuba which included banning travel to the island by most U.S. citizens, tightening the economic embargo, and creating the anti-Castro broadcasting station "Radio Martí." Renewed U.S. attempts to isolate Cuba have largely failed, however, and only the U.S. government maintains unchanged the hostility of the past.

3

Nicaragua: Where's the Threat?

> We must prevent consolidation of a Sandinista regime in Nicaragua....If we cannot prevent that, we have to anticipate the partition of Central America. Such a development would then force us to man a new military front line of the East-West conflict, right here on our continent.
>
> **—Undersecretary of Defense Fred Iklé, September 1983**[1]

The threat of communism made its first appearance as a rationalization for U.S. policy toward Nicaragua during the 1920s, when the Soviet beachhead was said to be centered in Mexico. But the practice of "big stick" politics was already old. The United States had previously intervened in Nicaragua many times, economically, politically, and militarily.

One of the military men who carried out U.S. policy early in this century was Marine Corps Major General Smedley D. Butler. Twice wounded in action and twenty times decorated, Smedley Butler was also one of the few Americans to be twice awarded the Congressional Medal of Honor. His example is still held up to recruits as the ideal for a Marine officer. But after retiring from active duty, Butler wrote bitterly about the uses to which his service had been put:

> War is a racket. Our stake in that racket has never been greater in all our peace-time history.

Cutting a Switch for a Bad Boy
Source: McKee Barclay, *Baltimore Sun,* 1910

It may seem odd for me, a military man, to adopt such a comparison. Truthfulness compels me to. I spent 33 years and 4 months in active service as a member of our country's most agile military force—the Marine Corps....

I helped make Mexico and especially Tampico safe for American oil interests in 1914. I helped make Haiti and Cuba a decent place for the National City Bank boys to collect revenues in. I helped in the raping of half a dozen Central American republics for the benefit of Wall Street. The record of racketeering is long. I helped purify Nicaragua for the international banking house of Brown Brothers in 1909-12. I brought light to the Dominican Republic for

American sugar interests in 1916. I helped make Honduras "right" for American fruit companies in 1903....

Looking back on it, I feel I might have given Al Capone a few hints. The best *he* could do was to operate his racket in three city districts. We Marines operated on three *continents.*[2]

Butler commanded a marine detachment sent to Nicaragua in 1910, seven years before the Russian revolution brought the Soviet Union into existence. Here is a glimpse of how he managed that intervention:

> Dr. Madris [the president of Nicaragua] grew cold toward the Nicaraguan investments of Brown Bros. and Seligman & Co. Another revolution immediately "occurred" and our State Department sent a representative to see that the revolution was successful. Near Bluefields was the property of a large American gold mine, whose stock was owned mainly by Pittsburgh financiers and partly by the then Secretary of State, Philander C. Knox. President Madris refused to recognize the validity of the gold mining concession and 225 Marines immediately were dispatched to Bluefields to "protect American lives and property." I commanded those Marines and in order to be sure that there was an American life to protect in Bluefields I made certain the local American consul was on the job. There wasn't another American in miles....[3]

In 1985, President Reagan said that Nicaragua represents "an unusual and extraordinary threat to the national security and foreign policy of the United States." The menace, according to the president, results from Nicaragua's "aggressive activities" and its allegiance to the Soviet camp in the East-West conflict.[4] To cope with this alleged threat, the Reagan administration in 1985 declared a national emergency and an economic embargo against Nicaragua; long before, in 1981, it had begun organizing the contra (counterrevolutionary) forces which the administration continues to arm and sponsor in a bloody war aimed at the overthrow of the Nicaraguan government.

On July 19, 1979 the revolutionary government took office in Nicaragua, ending forty-three years of corrupt and brutal Somoza family rule. The Somoza regime had been noted for its subservience to U.S. foreign policy, and it actively assisted such U.S. operations as the 1961 invasion of Cuba at the Bay of Pigs. This era came to a close when the Nicaraguan National Guard, defender of the Somoza dynasty and a legacy from the U.S. military occupation which lasted until 1933, was defeated and scattered in a widespread popular insurrection led by the Sandinista National Liberation Front (FSLN).

The Soviet Union and the established pro-Soviet Nicaraguan communist party—the Partido Socialista Nicaraguense, or PSN—played minimal roles in the overthrow of Somoza. According to the Jacobsen report, a study commissioned by the U.S. State Department,

> The Nicaraguan revolution caught Moscow off-guard. The Moscow-line Socialist Party had judged that the situation was not ripe for revolution, and had consequently condemned the Sandinistas' insurrectionary strategy as adventurist.[5]

Not until late in 1978 did the PSN create an armed group to join the insurrection, and the decision to unite its efforts with those of the Sandinistas came still later. As a result, the communists had little standing in the revolutionary government. The PSN still exists, and in the 1984 elections it received 1.3 percent of the vote.

The anti-Somoza movement in Nicaragua did have some outside assistance. Cuban political support for the Sandinistas goes back many years; Cuba provided a haven for the revolutionaries and gave them small amounts of material help. But Cuban military aid was not decisive in the victory. Significant quantities of arms from outside did not reach the Nicaraguan rebels until the late 1970s, and then they came in larger quantities from Venezuela, Panama and Costa Rica than from Cuba. Mexico and Colombia also provided political and material support.[6]

U.S. economic and military aid had flowed steadily to Nicaragua until 1977, when President Carter suspended the aid because of Somoza's abysmal human rights record. The human rights standards were not consistently applied, however, and in 1978 Washington resumed economic aid despite the lack of any significant improvement. As the fall of Somoza became more and more inevitable, the Carter administration made several attempts to modify Nicaragua's revolutionary process. First it tried to arrange Somoza's resignation and orchestrate a successor regime preserving the National Guard. When this proved impossible, it worked to secure a transition government with minimum Sandinista influence. Finally, the United States proposed a "peacekeeping force" from the Organization of American States (OAS) in order to prevent a Sandinista military victory. These attempts were too late and too transparent to be politically realistic, and the United States did not succeed in isolating the Sandinistas from their more conservative anti-Somoza allies.[7]

When the successful "final offensive" defeated the Guard and brought the Sandinistas to power, Nicaragua's new government found the country in a desperate situation. Almost two percent of the population had died in the insurrection, and many more were wounded. Material damage from the war was great, perhaps half a billion dollars, while foreign debt came to $1.6 billion. The latter amounted to approximately $640 per capita, three times the median annual income of the poorer 50 percent of the population. (The average GNP per capita for all Nicaraguans was slightly over $800.) The national treasury had been looted, while the Somoza family had accumulated a fortune of over $500 million.[8] Along with the material damage, many of Nicaragua's normal social structures had also been swept away. The problems of reconstruction were huge and the available resources few.

Faced with the reality of a Sandinista victory, the Carter administration decided to offer Nicaragua limited U.S. assistance, evidently hoping to prevent the radicalization and dependence on the Soviet Union which had occurred in Cuba, and to influence Nicaragua in directions acceptable to the United States. A sharply divided Congress approved $75 million in economic aid early in 1980, but only after making numerous changes in the administration's request. Most of the aid, $70 million, was in the form of credits rather than grants, with 60 percent earmarked for the private sector. The use of the aid was restricted in other ways as well; for example, no U.S. funds could be used for any educational project involving Cubans, and one percent of the money had to be spent to publicize U.S. generosity. Disbursement did not begin until September 1980.[9]

In keeping with its stated policy of non-alignment, Nicaragua set out soon after the revolutionary victory to expand and diversify its trade relations and aid sources. Cuba quickly sent teachers and medical personnel, followed by economic, technical and military advisers; it was the only socialist country to provide significant aid during the revolution's first eight months. However, aid was soon forthcoming from many parts of the Western world. Mexico became Nicaragua's largest single backer, having provided over $500 million in credits by mid-1984. Other countries supplying important help included France, West Germany, Spain, Holland, Italy, Sweden and Canada. Multilateral institutions such as the World Bank and U.N. agencies also played a major role, especially in the early years.[10] (See Figure 2.)

The Soviet Union and other socialist countries (with the exception of Cuba) were slower to become involved, but before long they too were providing assistance to Nicaragua. While important, this aid

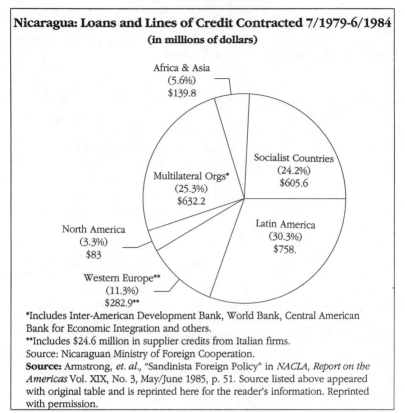

Nicaragua: Loans and Lines of Credit Contracted 7/1979-6/1984
(in millions of dollars)

Africa & Asia
(5.6%)
$139.8

Multilateral Orgs*
(25.3%)
$632.2

Socialist Countries
(24.2%)
$605.6

North America
(3.3%)
$83

Latin America
(30.3%)
$758.

Western Europe**
(11.3%)
$282.9**

*Includes Inter-American Development Bank, World Bank, Central American Bank for Economic Integration and others.
**Includes $24.6 million in supplier credits from Italian firms.
Source: Nicaraguan Ministry of Foreign Cooperation.
Source: Armstrong, *et. al.,* "Sandinista Foreign Policy" in *NACLA, Report on the Americas* Vol. XIX, No. 3, May/June 1985, p. 51. Source listed above appeared with original table and is reprinted here for the reader's information. Reprinted with permission.

was limited in extent. The State Department's Jacobsen report describes Soviet economic aid in some detail, and comments:

> aid from Western Europe and UN agencies has been even more substantial, and hence crucial. Furthermore, it must also be said that in the context of her overall aid to Third World nations, Moscow's commitment to Nicaragua is modest.[11]

The importance of economic aid from the socialist world grew, however, as Western and multilateral sources reduced their assistance during the 1980s. This reduction came, at least in part, in response to increasing pressure from the United States, which made strong efforts to block loans to Nicaragua from international agencies. For example, the Inter-American Development Bank (IDB) has made no loan to Nicaragua since 1982. In a January 1985 letter to the IDB's president, Secretary of State George Shultz urged denial of a loan requested by

Nicaragua to develop its private-sector agriculture. In his letter Shultz implied that IDB approval of the loan request could jeopardize future U.S. support for the bank. A senior IDB official stated in 1985, "I have never seen such political pressure on the bank as in the last four years."[12]

In January 1981, during its last days in office, the Carter administration suspended payment to Nicaragua of the $15 million remaining from the $75 million aid fund created the previous year. This action was based on the charge that Nicaragua was supporting the guerrillas in El Salvador with arms, men and supplies. The available evidence indicates that arms were sent from Nicaraguan territory to the Salvadoran revolutionaries in late 1980 and January 1981, in support of their unsuccessful "final offensive" launched before the Reagan administration took office. The evidence also shows that such aid largely stopped early in 1981. (This issue is discussed in detail in the following chapter.) The incoming Reagan administration, however, continued to accuse the Nicaraguan government of extensive arms shipments to El Salvador, turned the aid suspension into a permanent cancellation and quickly began to organize the remnants of Somoza's National Guard into the counterrevolutionary forces now known as contras.

Accusations Against the Sandinistas

The Reagan administration's hostility to Nicaragua has been accompanied by a wide spectrum of accusations, not just the charge that Nicaragua arms the Salvadoran revolution. The accusations divide roughly into two categories: "external" charges that Nicaragua is a threat to peace, and "internal" charges of anti-democratic practices. The latter include accusations that the Nicaraguan government is a massive violator of human rights, suppressing religion and committing genocide against the Miskito Indians. Nicaragua's 1984 election is described as a "Soviet-style sham," and President Daniel Ortega is portrayed as a dictator. The Nicaraguan government is said to be systematically destroying the private sector of the economy. Both parts of the indictment are repeated in *The Challenge to Democracy in Central America,* published by the administration in the autumn of 1986.[13]

Strictly speaking, the "internal" charges are not relevant to the question of U.S. security, and perhaps it should not be necessary to discuss them here. The United States does not make war on other

Children learning to read during the literacy campaign. Copyright
Pat Gouvdis, 1986.

countries, either covertly or openly, simply because their governments
abuse the civil liberties of the citizens or mismanage the economy. Even
if the Reagan administration's charges against Nicaragua were fully accurate—and they are not—the charges would neither explain nor justify U.S. policy. Nevertheless, the incessant accusations of
anti-democratic practices in Nicaragua have been effective in reducing
U.S. public sympathy for the revolution and increasing acceptance of
the administration's war policy. Although a full analysis of the widely-
scattered U.S. charges is beyond the scope of this study,[14] several aspects
of the indictment deserve brief comment.

First, it is noteworthy that the positive achievements of the
Nicaraguan revolution are minimized or totally ignored in all official
U.S. statements and in much of the U.S. media coverage as well.
Nicaragua was honored by UNESCO for its 1980 National Literacy Campaign, which reduced the nation's illiteracy rate among adults from over
50 percent to below 15 percent. The revolution has brought health services, especially preventive medicine, to thousands of Nicaraguans who
previously had no such care, and in 1982 the World Health Organization awarded Nicaragua its prize for the most significant achievement
in public health by a Third World nation. Land reform is a third way in
which many rural Nicaraguans have gained from the revolution.
Women now have equal social and economic rights under Nicaraguan

law, including the laws of Agrarian Reform which changed the traditional practice of awarding land titles only to male heads of households. Women have also benefitted from innovative legal programs, child care services and other aspects of the "women's revolution within the revolution." Any evaluation of the Nicaraguan revolution which ignores these and other achievements is distorted at best.[15]

Second, Nicaragua's record on human rights, continually criticized by the United States, is actually far better than that of neighboring countries whose governments the United States supports. It is true, for example, that the Nicaraguan government and armed forces acted badly toward Miskito and other Indian groups during the early years of the revolution, leading to serious problems still festering despite recent progress toward a solution. But at their worst these abuses cannot be compared to the situation which prevailed in Guatemala during those same years, where repression and mass murder of citizens, especially Indians, took place on an appalling scale. In its July 1985 report on Nicaragua, the independent human rights organization Americas Watch made this point clearly:

> In Nicaragua there is no systematic practice of forced disappearances, extrajudicial killings or torture—as has been the case with the "friendly" armed forces of El Salvador....Nor has the government practiced elimination of cultural or ethnic groups, as the [Reagan] Administration frequently claims; indeed in this respect, as in most others, Nicaragua's record is by no means so bad as that of Guatemala, whose government the Administration consistently defends.[16]

And yet it is Nicaragua, and not Guatemala or El Salvador, which Mr. Reagan calls a "totalitarian dungeon." The latter two countries enjoy the support of the U.S. government, as do other nations worldwide whose human rights practices are abysmal, such as Turkey and South Africa.

Third, Nicaragua's economic system—a "mixed economy" which combines elements of state ownership or control with a large private sector—also cannot really be the reason for unremitting U.S. hostility. The United States maintains good relations with socialist countries such as Yugoslavia, and is now planning to furnish both military equipment and nuclear technology to the world's most populous communist nation, the People's Republic of China. And despite the "evil empire" rhetoric of the past, the United States supplies grain and other products

Above and right: Nicaraguan's celebrating the birth of their constitution. John Lamperti.

to its socialist superpower rival, the Soviet Union, with whom in December 1987 the U.S. signed important arms control agreement.

Fourth, U.S. actions toward Nicaragua appear designed to wors-
en the very problems about which the United States complains. For example, attempting to disrupt and discredit Nicaragua's elections, as the
Reagan administration did, is no way to encourage democracy there.
A delegation of U.S. scholars from the Latin American Studies Association observed the 1984 Nicaraguan election and gave them generally
high marks for honesty and fairness. But the delegation's report points
out that

> The range of options available to the Nicaraguan voter on most
> issues was broad, but it would have been even broader if the U.S.
> government had not succeeded in persuading or pressuring key
> opposition leaders to boycott or withdraw from the election. We
> found that the behavior of U.S. officials during the six months
> preceding the elections was clearly interventionist, apparently
> designed to delegitimize the Nicaraguan electoral process by
> making sure that the FSLN had no externally credible opposition
> to run against.[17]

Six other parties did run in the elections in addition to the FSLN,
and together the opposition parties won thirty-five of the ninety-six
seats in the National Assembly. This assembly has since overseen the

CONSTITUCION:
nuestro compromiso
con el futuro

PARA
QUÉ?

PARA QUE LA TIERRA SEA DE
QUIEN LA TRABAJE

drafting, revision, and enactment (in January 1987) of a new Nicaraguan constitution which, at least on paper, provides strong guarantees for human rights and democratic procedures.[18]

The Reagan administration claims that it favors human rights in Nicaragua, and it frequently condemns Nicaragua's "unnecessary" military buildup. However, since 1981 the administration has promoted and sponsored a covert war against Nicaragua by means of the contra forces. This war has involved innumerable direct attacks on the civilian population, leading to thousands of casualties.[19] The war has been a major factor in Nicaragua's military buildup; it is difficult to imagine that it could have had any other effect. In addition, Nicaragua's need to devote resources to defense has severely restricted its positive programs for human development and contributed to coercive measures such as the military draft. Thus U.S. policies have in reality impeded Nicaragua's steps toward democracy, degraded the human rights of its citizens, and made its further militarization inevitable.

It seems clear, then, that the Reagan administration's accusations against Nicaragua have little to do with any U.S. concern for human rights or distress over Nicaragua's allegedly anti-democratic practices, and a great deal to do with the realities of U.S. politics. The purpose of the campaign is to ease public acceptance of a militaristic and aggressive policy against a small, impoverished country attempting to construct a new society.

Nicaragua's Armed Forces: Threat or Defense?

The administration insists that an ominous and threatening military buildup is taking place in Nicaragua. *The Sandinista Military Build-up*, a joint State and Defense Department document issued in 1985, states:

> The Sandinistas realized that, as they proceeded with their secret agenda of fostering a Marxist-Leninist regime and exporting revolution throughout the region, they would encounter growing resistance from the nations of the region and from the Nicaraguan people themselves. The Sandinistas sought to develop a powerful military force which could intimidate their neighbors and suppress domestic opposition, thereby providing them with a secure base for their subversive activities.

The Soviet Union's geopolitical plotting is said to lie behind the Nicaraguan revolution, and this poses the most serious problems of all:

> Consolidation of the Sandinista regime in Nicaragua is a serious concern to the United States, for the Soviet Union can and does use Nicaragua to carry out Soviet policies in Central America....As the Soviets seek to foment further instability and revolution in Central America, they now have a willing accomplice in Sandinista-controlled Nicaragua.[20]

Another 1985 State/Defense publication, *The Soviet-Cuban Connection in Central America and the Caribbean*, strikes a similar note but puts greater emphasis on the role of Cuba:

> The decisions of the Soviet Union and Cuba to make this investment in Nicaragua indicate that Soviet leaders consider Nicaragua an important complement to Cuba in the Soviet strategy to increase pressure on the United States in the Caribbean Basin.[21]

The administration repeated and amplified these themes in its 1986 publication *The Challenge to Democracy in Central America*.

These documents in which the administration states its indictment of Nicaragua are highly biased. They do not mention that Nicaragua has been at war for most of the years since its revolution—at war against armed forces organized, equipped, trained, and paid by the United

States. They do not mention the air attacks against Nicaragua or the mining of its harbors by the CIA—although they state that Nicaragua has acquired anti-aircraft weapons and that the "Sandinista navy" operates six small minesweepers. The documents do not mention the continual, illegal U.S. flights over Nicaraguan territory, even though they are themselves heavily loaded with aerial photos of Nicaragua for which no sources are given. *The Sandinista Military Build-up* describes Nicaragua's use of the draft as if it were some unprecedented evil; in fact, Guatemala, El Salvador and Honduras all conscript their soldiers and the United States has itself drafted young men into its army during many years both of peace and war. Finally, and remarkably, while arguing the legality of the U.S. intervention in Nicaragua, *Challenge to Democracy* never mentions the clearcut judgement by the International Court of Justice (the World Court) that U.S. actions against Nicaragua violate international law.

There is, of course, no question that Nicaragua has greatly built up its armed forces since the revolution. When Somoza was overthrown, the Nicaraguan military was left in shambles. In 1980 a U.S. government report stated that Nicaragua's armed forces would have to be completely rebuilt:

> To an even greater degree than other elements of government, the Nicaraguan defense establishment was swept away. Nothing remains except for some small arms and the battered remnants of other equipment, all of it battle-scarred and most of it fit for little more than salvage. The armed forces of Nicaragua must be entirely rebuilt, both in personnel and equipment.[22]

The Nicaraguan government describes the purpose and structure of Nicaragua's reconstructed armed forces as defensive, not offensive. Defense Minister Humberto Ortega has specifically denied that Nicaragua is preparing for external adventures:

> Our system for the military defense of the country, whose nucleus is the Sandinista People's Army, has an eminently defensive character and is not aimed toward carrying out military campaigns outside of our own territory.[23]

Private assessments within the U.S. government have found Nicaragua's claim of a defensive military posture to be credible. According to the *Wall Street Journal*, a "classified U.S. intelligence report" prepared late in 1984 says of Nicaragua's military that "the overall buildup is primarily defense-oriented, and much of the recent effort has been devoted to

improving counterinsurgency capabilities." The same article quotes
Secretary of State George Shultz's accusation that the Nicaraguan army
"far exceeds anything remotely needed for defense in Central America,"
but states that

> The classified U.S. intelligence report prepared late last year con-
> tradicts Secretary Shultz. And figures in the report suggest the in-
> crease in Soviet aid to Nicaragua may have been prompted by the
> escalation of the CIA-backed contra war.[24]

Nicaragua clearly has no ability to threaten the United States
militarily; in particular, it has neither an air force nor a navy capable of
operating much beyond Nicaragua's own borders. Dangers to the
United States itself are entirely hypothetical, depending on the possible
future existence of Soviet military bases within Nicaraguan territory. No
such bases exist now, however, and their establishment is highly unlikely.

First, the Nicaraguan government has repeatedly stated that it has
no desire or intention of allowing any foreign bases within the country.
It insists that Nicaragua's foreign policy is based on non-alignment and
that as a matter of principle no foreign bases are wanted. Government
leaders stress that the revolution is being constructed for the Nicaraguan
people and not to benefit any outsiders, even allies who provide aid.
Even if such official declarations in themselves carry little weight, the
stated policy is a plausible one. Nicaraguan leaders realize that Soviet
bases would be magnets for U.S. attack rather than a protection.

Second, there is also no evidence that the Soviet Union wants
military bases in Nicaragua or the obligations which would come with
them. The Soviet government has repeatedly emphasized Nicaragua's
need to be able to defend itself. Both Soviet and Cuban leaders have
been extremely cautious about making promises to Nicaragua, giving
assurances of their wholehearted political support and "solidarity" but
never offering any treaty or other commitment which would obligate
them to intervene directly if Nicaragua were attacked.[25]

Finally, the United States has had and continues to have the possibility of turning Nicaragua's no-foreign-bases policy into a firm treaty
obligation with ample provisions for verification. This could be done
in the context of a security treaty for the whole region as proposed by
the Contadora group of nations, or through a bilateral agreement.
Nicaragua has declared itself willing to meet legitimate U.S. security
concerns in a peace settlement and has repeatedly expressed a desire

to negotiate its differences with the United States, but the U.S. government has declined to work toward such a settlement.[26]

Military Capabilities

What are Nicaragua's actual military capabilities? Its active-duty forces currently number about 75,000 men and women, plus 44,000 in the inactive reserves and unmobilized militia units. (For comparison, the active-duty forces of Guatemala number about 43,000, of El Salvador 49,000, and the figure for Honduras is about 22,000.)[27] The U.S. military suggests as a rule of thumb that a successful counterinsurgency war requires ten government soldiers to every guerrilla. By this standard, in view of U.S. claims that there are some 20,000 active contra fighters, the size of Nicaragua's army is modest.

The main component of Nicaragua's army is the infantry, but it also has armor and artillery. *The Sandinista Military Build-up* puts the number of tanks at "more than 110" T-54 and T-55 medium tanks, plus "about 30" PT-60 light tanks. In addition, there are said to be "more than 200 armored vehicles," mostly armored personnel carriers, for a total of over 340 vehicles. The report asserts that "The growth of EPS's [the Nicaraguan army's] artillery force has been equally dramatic," and states that this force includes twenty-four each of Soviet-made 152 mm and 122 mm howitzers, plus multiple rocket launchers and many smaller guns. There are also numerous military trucks and other support vehicles.[28] Do these forces constitute an offensive threat, as the Reagan administration asserts?

One military expert who believes otherwise is Lt. Colonel Edward King (ret.). Col. King served as a combat and staff officer of the U.S. Army, and was liaison to the Joint Chiefs of Staff from the Interamerican Defense Council. More recently he has been associate director of the Federation of American Scientists. King has made numerous trips to Central America and has talked with members of the Nicaraguan armed forces ranging from Defense Minister Humberto Ortega to private soldiers, as well as with contra leaders, Salvadoran rebels, and officers of the Salvadoran and Honduran armies. His assessment of the situation differs radically from the administration's, and takes into account factors which the State and Defense Department publications omit.

For example, in 1984 Col. King visited the town of Somotillo in a region of Nicaragua which U.S. military experts agree would have to be the corridor for any armored attack on Honduras. Here is an excerpt from his report on this visit:

> There is no evidence around Somotillo or near the highway ap-
> proaching the border of large tank concentrations and offensive
> preparations. No bridge exists over which tanks could cross the
> Negro river into Honduras. Such a crossing would require the for-
> ward movement of heavy bridging equipment or ferries, both of
> which could be readily detected by U.S. intelligence surveillance....
>
> The two roads that run north from Managua around each side of
> Lake Managua are not suitable for the rapid sustained movement
> of the tanks or large numbers of heavy supply vehicles needed in
> offensive operations. The narrow and badly maintained road from
> the port of Corinto to Somotillo...is not adequate for concentrated
> use by heavy fuel tank vehicles....
>
> On the basis of observable tank and troop deployments, the con-
> dition of the tanks themselves, the nature of the terrain and road
> network, and the non-appearance of logistic facilities for offensive
> operations, it appears that there is very little evidence in Nicaragua
> to support the frequently voiced possibility of any type of offen-
> sive operation against Honduras by the Sandinista Army. The San-
> dinista armed forces are just not positioned, equipped or supplied
> in a sufficient manner to undertake an attack against Honduras.[29]

In another report, Col. King describes in some detail what would actually be involved in a Nicaraguan tank attack on Honduras. It be-comes clear that such an attack is not a realistic possibility:

> Once a realistic appraisal is made of the probable outcome of a
> Sandinista offensive against Honduras, El Salvador or Costa Rica—
> one that considers Nicaragua's lack of a trained officer corps, a
> national mobilization or production base, sufficient fuel, as well
> as the absence of an adequate capability in the logistical, medical
> and maintenance services necessary for sustained field combat
> operations—it becomes highly unlikely, if not impossible, to
> believe that Sandinistas would ever seriously contemplate such a
> disastrous course of action.[30]

Another military officer skeptical of the Nicaraguan threat is Lt. Col. John Buchanan (ret.), a twenty-two-year veteran of the Marine Corps. In September 1982, Col. Buchanan testified to a congressional subcommittee that:

the Reagan administration has distorted the facts to present an exaggerated picture of the military strength of Nicaragua. In this way, the Administration hopes to convince the U.S. public and the world that Nicaragua is the primary threat to peace in Central America. From what I have seen...this is simply not true.

For example, the much-vaunted threat of the Soviet-built T-55 tanks in Nicaragua is really a hollow threat, given the terrible mechanical performance of these tanks and the rugged terrain in the area which is totally unsuited to tank warfare. No Honduran officer to whom I have talked disputes that fact.[31]

While the numbers have changed since 1982, Buchanan's assessment of the threat of invasion by Nicaragua remains the same.[32]

Air power is vital for any possible offensive, and U.S. intelligence has called Nicaragua's air force "one of the smallest and least capable in the region."[33] As of the fall of 1987, Nicaragua has no "first-line" combat aircraft—supersonic fighters or fighter-bombers. The Nicaraguan air force does have sixteen outdated U.S.- and Italian-built planes of marginal capability and condition—possibly useful in support of ground forces against the contras but outclassed for aerial combat and outnumbered by the much more modern planes of both Honduras and El Salvador. (This is true even without the current acquisition by Honduras of new high-performance combat aircraft.) Nicaragua also has around twenty fixed-wing transports. Nicaragua's most important military aircraft are its forty to fifty helicopters, especially the Mi-8/17 troop-carrying helicopters and ten to fifteen Mi-24/25 HIND attack helicopters obtained from the Soviet Union.[34] These are effective weapons for the contra war but, as Col. King comments, still they

are only helicopters and no match for El Salvador's A-37B's and Honduras' A-37B's and Super Mystéres, or the hundreds of U.S. carrier and land based high performance fighter-bombers in the region.[35]

Diplomats and military experts in the region agree that despite their value in a counterinsurgency role, these helicopters are not capable of much "force projection" beyond Nicaragua's borders and that "the Nicaraguan Air Force still does not pose a threat to nearby countries."[36]

Could the inferiority of Nicaragua's air force be quickly reversed? The U.S. government has repeatedly warned that advanced Soviet fighter aircraft were coming, but so far they have always been wrong. Without doubt Nicaraguan military leaders would like to add modern

fighter aircraft to their forces, and they insist that they have every right
to do so. But Nicaragua has chosen to be cautious, and in the hope of
cooling the regional arms race announced in February 1985 its intention not to acquire advanced jet aircraft.[37] (At the same time, Nicaragua
sent home a hundred Cuban military advisers.) In a May 1986 proposal
to the Contadora group Nicaragua specifically mentioned military
aircraft and airfields as a matter for negotiation. However, the Pentagon
stated in October 1986 that it planned to help Honduras acquire modern
combat planes to upgrade its air force, already far superior to
Nicaragua's. In May 1987 the White House announced that the United
States would supply Honduras with twelve F-5E jet fighters.[38]

The United States expresses concern about Nicaragua's improvement of its airport facilities. *The Sandinista Military Build-up* describes
the main example this way:

> In 1982, with Cuban and Soviet assistance, the Sandinistas began
> constructing the Punta Huete airfield in an isolated area northeast
> of Managua. The principle runway at Punta Huete is 10,000 feet
> in length, making it the longest military runway in Central America.
> When completed, it will be able to accommodate any aircraft in
> the Soviet-bloc inventory....
>
> Soviet reconnaissance planes flying out of Punta Huete would be
> able to fly missions along the U.S. Pacific Coast, just as they now
> reconnoiter the U.S. Atlantic Coast from Cuba.[39]

The Punta Huete airport was actually begun under the Somoza
regime, with U.S. technical assistance. Somoza, like the present leadership, wanted to provide the Nicaraguan Air Force with a base separate
from the civilian international airport serving Managua, which now must
perform both functions. (The desirability of the separation was underlined in 1983 when CIA-supplied contra planes attacked Managua airport and bombed the passenger terminal.) It is true that the new
runways at Punta Huete could handle any Soviet plane, just as runways
built by the United States in Honduras can handle any U.S. military
aircraft. It is also true that the Soviets could fly reconnaissance missions
from Punta Huete if the Nicaraguans chose to let them. But Soviet planes
are already patrolling off the U.S. Pacific Coast from bases located within
the USSR's territory on the Kamchatka Peninsula. In this respect as in
others, hypothetical bases in Nicaragua would offer the Soviet Union
little which it does not already have.

A Nicaraguan view of the Threat. Róger Sánchez.

If Nicaragua has no offensive capability or intention, finally, what purpose does its military buildup serve? As Col. Edward King discovered, "Once the origin and the mission of the Sandinista armed forces are examined, the answer is obvious: to defend the revolution, not to export it."[40]

Why Do They "Defend the Revolution" With Soviet Guns?

U.S. government publications such as *The Sandinista Military Build-up* accuse the Sandinistas of plotting from the start to turn their country into a Soviet-Cuban military outpost:

> Contrary to Sandinista assertions that their military build-up has been the result of "counterrevolutionary activities" and "foreign aggression," the blueprint for the creation of a powerful combined arms force...was drawn at least 2 years before significant armed opposition arose. The Sandinistas planned the build-up at a time when the National Guard had been routed, the revolution had broad popular support, and the international community was highly supportive—with the United States leading the efforts to provide economic assistance.[41]

This accusation is misleading on at least two counts. First, it suggests that the early years of the revolution were peaceful and unthreatened. In reality, the Nicaraguan revolution had to deal with internal disorder, armed attacks, and the threat of counterrevolution from the very beginning. Some 3,000 members of Somoza's National Guard had crossed into Honduras and been welcomed there. Rumors of a counterrevolutionary invasion were widespread in Managua in August 1979, and there were cross-border attacks by bands of the ex-Guardsmen. Border incidents led to deteriorating relations with Honduras, including at times fear of actual war. By 1980 several groups of contras were raiding from Honduran territory and had proclaimed in Tegucigalpa, the Honduran capital, their intention to overthrow the Sandinistas. Seven teachers in Nicaragua's celebrated 1980 literacy campaign were killed by contra "freedom fighters." There were also pockets of Somocista resistance inside Nicaragua, as well as occasional violence from ultra-leftist groups and from common criminals.[42]

Second, it is hardly surprising that Nicaraguan leaders foresaw the danger of much greater threats in the future. They had convincing historical examples to guide them: the U.S. overthrow of the Arbenz government in Guatemala (1954), attacks on the Cuban revolution starting in 1960, invasion of the Dominican Republic (1965), U.S. complicity in military coups in Brazil (1964), Chile (1973) and elsewhere—plus the long history of U.S. military interventions in Nicaragua itself since the 1850s. Moreover, the Republican Party platform in 1980 expressed

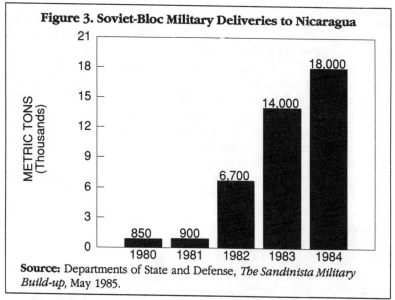

Figure 3. Soviet-Bloc Military Deliveries to Nicaragua

METRIC TONS (Thousands)

- 1980: 850
- 1981: 900
- 1982: 6,700
- 1983: 14,000
- 1984: 18,000

Source: Departments of State and Defense, *The Sandinista Military Build-up,* May 1985.

strong hostility to the Nicaraguan revolution and implied future attempts to overthrow it.

But why did Nicaragua turn to the Soviet Union and Cuba? Again U.S. government charges are misleading. Nicaragua did not receive large amounts of Soviet-bloc military equipment until 1982, after the U.S./contra war was well underway and after the United States had begun major military buildups in El Salvador and Honduras. During 1979 and 1980 the USSR and its allies sent Nicaragua arms worth $12 million—defensive weapons such as short-range anti-tank and anti-aircraft guns and missiles. In 1981 arms shipments increased to 937 tons of material worth about $45 million; nearly all of this was accounted for by twenty-five or twenty-six secondhand T-55 tanks from Algeria. The tanks weigh thirty-six tons each.[43] (See Figure 3.)

During its first two years, the new Nicaraguan government tried hard to obtain military assistance from the West, including the United States. These efforts failed because the U.S. government intentionally frustrated Nicaragua's efforts to get arms from any Western source. Consequently, the Soviet connection was cemented. Thus the United States helped bring about the situation about which it now complains bitterly.[44]

In September 1979, two months after the revolutionary government took power, Nicaraguan leaders approached the United States with requests for both economic and military aid. Their needs were clear and some members of the Carter administration were sympathetic to meeting both requests, reasoning in part that if the United States did not help, the Cubans and Soviets would. But the administration ran into difficulty getting a modest economic aid package through Congress and was not able or willing to insist on military assistance; its proposal for $5.5 million in military aid was removed from the bill in committee. Despite U.S. government recognition that the Nicaraguan army would have to be rebuilt almost from scratch, the United States offered only token assistance: $3,000 for binoculars and compasses, plus $20,000 to allow six Nicaraguan officers to tour several U.S. army bases.

The United States did make one other offer: to train Nicaraguan officers at the U.S. Army's "School of the Americas" in Panama. This school had trained military personnel for many right-wing Latin American regimes, and among its graduates were 4,693 members of Somoza's National Guard, more than from any other country. As the school's Public Affairs Officer acknowledged, "So many Somoza men trained here that I am sure it will take time before the Sandinistas decide to send anyone." He was right; the Nicaraguans turned down the offer.[45]

Having failed to obtain U.S. military assistance in the form of grants, the Sandinistas then tried to buy arms in Western Europe and the United States. In January 1981 two Nicaraguan officers were arrested in Texas while trying to purchase and fly home two Huey helicopters, items on the U.S. Munitions Control List which cannot be exported without government permission. They were charged, ironically, with violating the U.S. Neutrality Act.[46]

At first, European arms suppliers were no more helpful. Nicaragua's difficulties in buying arms contrast sharply with the experience of Guatemala; when the United States halted military aid in 1978 due to human rights abuses, the Guatemalan government had no trouble arranging new sources of material, principally from Israel.[47] But Nicaragua found an opening following the French elections of May 1981, and in December of that year the new French government signed an agreement allowing Nicaragua to purchase military equipment worth $15.8 million. Included in the deal were two helicopters, two coastal patrol boats, forty-five troop-carrying trucks, a number of rocket launchers and their ammunition, plus training for ten pilots and ten naval officers.

The agreement with France was small even by Nicaragua's standards and tiny by those of France, which had just concluded a $2.5 billion deal with Saudi Arabia. Nevertheless, the Reagan administration was outraged. Secretary of State Alexander Haig called it "a stab in the back." The United States applied intense political and economic pressure, with evident effect. Delivery of the equipment to Nicaragua stalled, and there have been no further arms sales by France. President Mitterand privately assured Reagan in March 1982 that delivery of the helicopters "would face indefinite delays."[48]

An even smaller agreement, worth $5.5 million, was concluded with Holland in 1983. Its purpose was to improve the port defenses at Corinto, and it is the last recorded Nicaraguan success in obtaining military assistance from nations allied with the United States.[49] With these exceptions the door to Western military aid was firmly closed, and the Soviet Union and its allies became the only sources of supply for Nicaragua's military needs. This fact, and whatever degree of dependence it implies, were the direct result of decisions made in Washington.

*   *   *

The question remains, what are we afraid of in the Nicaraguan revolution? One U.S. observer describes the revolution as "something new and innovative—a blend of nationalism, pragmatic Marxism, and Catholic humanism," and suggests "that is precisely why it was so threatening to conservative ideologues in the United States."[50] Can it be that ideas and not guns are the essence of the threat?

Nicaragua has broken ranks; it no longer marches to Washington's tune. So far the United States has refused to accept Nicaragua's declaration of independence. Current U.S. policy is strikingly at odds with the more courageous thinking of a former president of the United States, thinking which his own administration did not always put into practice:

> Any nation's right to a form of government and an economic system of its own choosing is inalienable. Any nation's attempt to dictate to other nations their form of government is indefensible.

—Dwight David Eisenhower
President of the United States, 1953-1961

El Salvador: Communist Aggression or Civil War?

Lacking broad popular support, the guerrillas continue to be a potent military force because of the extensive support they receive from Nicaragua, Cuba, other communist countries such as Vietnam, and radical regimes such as Libya. The unification of the Salvadoran guerrillas was coordinated by Fidel Castro.

—**Departments of State and Defense, 1985**[1]

In an interview with *Newsweek* magazine early in 1981, then Ambassador to the United Nations Jeane Kirkpatrick insisted that the violence in El Salvador was not caused by social injustice—"a situation that has existed for decades"—but by "the introduction of arms from the outside."[2] That idea has been basic for U.S. policy in Central America since 1981. Here is a very different picture of the situation:

Fifty years of lies, fifty years of injustice, fifty years of frustration. This is a history of people starving to death, living in misery. For fifty years the same people had all the power, all the money, all the jobs, all the education, all the opportunities. Those who did not have anything tried to take it away from those who had everything. But there were no democratic systems available to them, so they have radicalized themselves, have resorted to violence. And of course this second group, the rich, do not want to give up anything, so they are fighting.

This second statement comes not from a revolutionary or leftist but from José Napoleón Duarte, now El Salvador's president. Reporter Raymond Bonner, who interviewed Duarte in 1980, was surprised by his sympathetic explanation for the revolution, and adds:

> But what struck me more...was what he [Duarte] had not said. He had said nothing about Castro or Cuba. He had not mentioned the Sandinistas or Nicaragua. There was no talk of the cold war and the Soviet Union. (Duarte was to raise those themes later, when they reflected the views of the Reagan administration in Washington.) What Duarte was saying was that the revolution had been caused and fueled by the conditions in El Salvador.[3]

Duarte's "fifty years" leads back to the Indian and peasant rebellion of 1932 and the great army massacre and repression which followed it. Among the rebellion's organizers was Augustín Farabundo Martí, a self-described communist for whom the present-day guerrilla organization, the Farabundo Martí Front for National Liberation (FMLN), is named. Communists or not, Martí and his fellow revolutionaries were native Salvadorans. Their plans misfired badly and the uprising was quickly crushed by the Salvadoran army.

Historian Thomas Anderson has estimated that the number of civilians killed by the 1932 rebels "could not have been more than thirty-five" and the total number of casualties they inflicted, including soldiers, was under a hundred persons.[4] The Salvadoran army, however, killed tens of thousands of peasants in retribution; Martí himself was executed for his part in planning the uprising. General Hernández Martínez, who commanded the army during the brief fighting and the subsequent slaughter, became the strong man of the Salvadoran government and maintained himself in power until 1944.

El Salvador remained under nearly continuous military rule from 1932 until the 1980s. In 1960 reform-minded junior military officers succeeded in staging a coup; the junta they formed promised steps toward democracy including prompt, free elections. The United States, however, withheld its recognition—"apparently because the U.S. ambassador thought that some of the members admired Castro."[5] A second coup three months later installed a conservative colonel, Julio Adalberto Rivera, as head of yet another junta; Rivera became president a year later. One member of the ousted junta told Congress in 1976 that U.S. embassy officials had been hostile to the proposed reforms and openly supported the second coup.[6] In any case Washington immediately recognized Rivera's government, about which President Kennedy later

remarked that "governments of the civil-military type in El Salvador are the most effective in containing communism in Latin America."[7]

The legal political opposition to Colonel Rivera's "official" party did some serious organizing during the 1960s; the most prominent sector of this opposition was the Christian Democratic Party (PDC). The PDC's leader was José Napoleón Duarte. Duarte was elected mayor of San Salvador in 1964, reelected in 1966 and 1968 with large majorities, and became the party's presidential candidate for the election of 1972. It is generally believed that Duarte and his running-mate Guillermo Ungo were the true winners, but the government used blatant fraud to put its own candidates into office. The 1972 election is widely seen as a turning point. As Duarte himself has recently written, "it was during that period [after 1972] that the coming violence became inevitable...faith in the electoral process faded away. Many people concluded that the powers ruling El Salvador would never permit votes to defeat them. Change had to come by other means."[8] After 1972 the organizing of a mass resistance movement accelerated.

Another stolen election in 1977—Duarte calls it "the most blatant fraud El Salvador had ever known"[9]—reinforced the message and further polarized Salvadoran society. A peaceful mass protest against the fraud was attacked by security forces and many demonstrators—some accounts say more than two hundred—were shot down. The army was in control, peaceful demonstrations were increasingly met with massacres in the streets and countryside, and the growing guerrilla resistance seemed to many the only alternative to an increasingly intolerable status quo.

While extremes of poverty and injustice are an old story in El Salvador, in recent decades additional factors helped to form a revolutionary situation. One of these was a new current flowing within the Catholic church. In her study of the changing role of the church, Penny Lernoux says that the 1968 Bishops' conference in Medellín, Colombia "produced the Magna Carta of today's persecuted, socially-committed Church, and as such rates as one of the major political events of the century: it shattered the centuries-old alliance of Church, military, and the rich elites."[10]

The church—or parts of the church—adopted a "preferential option for the poor." It began to teach that social injustice is sinful, and that Christians should work to overcome it here on Earth. Just as important as the content of this message were the means chosen to communicate it—the formation of Christian Base Communities (CEBs). This process involves local organizing, bringing people together and en-

couraging them to take responsibility for their own religious lives. CEBs promote consciousness-raising and help develop leadership. These developments in the religious sphere strengthened organizing, protest and eventually rebellion in other areas of life as well.

One of the first to apply these ideas in El Salvador was Father José Inocencio Alas, who began organizing CEBs in Suchitoto in 1969. In 1970 he was chosen to deliver the church's position at a national agrarian reform congress. On the same day that he forcefully addressed the congress in favor of reform, Alas was kidnapped from the streets of San Salvador. He was found the next day in the mountains, beaten and drugged; strong protests from Bishop Rivera y Damas to the military authorities probably saved his life.[11] In 1974 peasants from Suchitoto's CEBs took part in organizing the first of El Salvador's mass popular organizations. Such organizations, uniting peasant groups and urban workers into effective coalitions for change, became another important part of El Salvador's political landscape in the second half of the 1970s.

By 1975 Father Alas was being denounced by the right as a subversive and a communist; after several other priests were murdered he left the country in 1977. By 1978 fifteen priests and nuns had been killed, as had many labor and peasant organizers, student leaders and others working nonviolently to change Salvadoran society. Still, not until Archbishop Oscar Romero was shot and killed in March 1980 while saying Mass, and three U.S. nuns and a lay missioner were raped and murdered in December of that year by the soldiers of the National Guard, did the repression begin to attract much notice in the United States.

The 1979 Coup

Despite the growing violence, El Salvador had one more chance for peaceful change. On October 15, 1979 a "young officers" group of a reformist bent led a coup which deposed the military president, General Humberto Romero. The successful conspirators established a combined military and civilian junta to provide top leadership, promised to work for major reforms, and persuaded some of El Salvador's ablest citizens to join the new government.

Three months later the chance was gone. Reform-minded elements in the new junta had been unable to gain control over the military and the security forces or to halt the violence against the population;

more people were killed in the first three weeks after the coup than in any three-week period of the previous regime.[12] Officially the United States supported human rights and social reform, but in practice the Carter administration's policies were inconsistent, and often undercut the civilian and military reformers in their power struggle against the traditional military leadership and the right.[13] The result was a complete failure to stop the repression.

On January 3 and 4, 1980, after the true balance of power became clear, all the civilian members of the junta and the cabinet resigned from the government. A few days later the Christian Democratic Party stepped in to preserve the formal civilian-military alliance, and a new junta was formed. But this second junta, like the first one, lacked the power it really needed to govern: control over the armed forces. One of the new civilian members, Héctor Dada, also resigned less than two months later, declaring that "We have not been able to stop the repression, and those committing acts of repression disrespectful of the authority of the Junta go unpunished." Within a month three cabinet ministers joined Dada in leaving the government. One of them explained it this way:

> This war, whose dead are, in the majority, peasants and militants of the popular organizations, reflects who the security forces and the Army consider their principal enemies.[14]

The Christian Democratic Party (PDC) held a convention in March 1980 to decide its course. Archbishop Romero called upon the Christian Democrats to withdraw from the government, stating that their presence was legitimizing the repression. The party nevertheless decided to remain, and José Napoleón Duarte replaced Héctor Dada in the junta. The decision split the PDC, and the members who walked out formed a new group, the Popular Social Christian Movement (MPSC). The MPSC soon allied itself with the recently-formed Democratic Revolutionary Front (FDR), a coalition of popular organizations which provided political leadership to the opposition movement.

The twice-revamped junta, like its predecessors, was unable to control the armed forces or to end the repression. Another shake-up in December 1980 ousted the pro-reform Colonel Arnoldo Majano and installed Duarte as president of the junta, where he served until the elections of March 1982. While 1980 had been a year of bloody repression, 1981 was even worse. That year some 12,500 Salvadoran civilians were victims of politically-motivated murder, according to the Archdiocesan legal aid office in San Salvador; most of those killings were carried out

Two Who Gave Their Lives

Oscar Arnulfo Romero, born in a remote Salvadoran village in 1917, was appointed Archbishop of San Salvador in 1977. In opposition to conservative currents within the Church, Archbishop Romero supported the right of peasants and workers to organize "base communities" and in the broad "popular organizations" which arose during the 1970s. As growing military and death-squad violence claimed the lives of thousands of Salvadorans, including priests who were his close friends, Romero spoke out more and more strongly on behalf of the Salvadoran people. In a March 1980 sermon, he issued a powerful appeal directly to members of the army and national guard, pleading with them, even ordering them in the name of God, to "Stop the repression!" The next day he was murdered while in the act of saying mass.

Courtesy Maryknoll Missioners, Wheater/El Salvador.

Enrique Alvarez Cordova, a member of an oligarchy family, enjoyed the advantages that go with great wealth. Educated in the United States (prep school and Rutgers University), he was a star on El Salvador's national basketball team and a ranked tennis player. But unlike many members of Central America's elite, Alvarez was also deeply dedicated to the advancement of his country. As a government official

Courtesy Maryknoll Missioners, Sandoval/U.S.

in 1968 he found that efforts at reform were thwarted by the opposition of the wealthy and the military. Alvarez served as minister of agriculture in the first junta after the 1979 coup, resigning with the other civilians when the junta proved unable to halt repression. In April 1980 he became the first head of the FDR, believing that "We have exhausted all peaceful means" for achieving social change. On November 27, a school where the FDR executive committee was meeting was raided by a hundred armed men, and Alvarez and five others were kidnapped. Their mutilated bodies were found a few days later.

by the military and security forces.[15] Nevertheless, at the year's end President Reagan certified to Congress that the Salvadoran government was making a "concerted and significant effort" to protect human rights and to end torture and murder by the military.

The U.S. Response

After the coup of October 1979, U.S. policy focused on the search for a viable political center. The Carter administration evidently believed the Christian Democrats could be the answer, and urged them to join the government in January 1980. The United States supported the reconstituted junta then and after its second reorganization in March, and applauded the junta's claim to be a government of the center, under fire from extremists of both the right and left. In reality the military and the right wing were steadily regaining power, and the opportunity for meaningful reform and an end to the violence was soon gone. Historian Thomas Anderson wrote in 1981:

> In El Salvador the moderate middle has virtually ceased to exist. Even moderates like Guillermo Ungo of the MNR have thrown in their lot with the leftist forces. The Christian Democrats were long thought to represent a "third force" between right and left that might bring change without revolution, but the PDC leaders lost contact with the mass organizations in the mid-1970s. Many Christian Democrats have joined the left.[16]

By this time a complex political struggle had evolved into civil war, a fact which the elections to be held in 1982 would not change. Early in 1980 the United States resumed "non-lethal" military aid; all military aid had been suspended since 1977. The resumption ignored a public plea from Archbishop Romero, who urged President Carter to withhold military aid since it would contribute to repression of the people. (A month after issuing that plea, on March 24, 1980, Romero himself was assassinated.) U.S. economic aid was also raised in 1980, and in January 1981, despite escalating repression and the murder by soldiers of four U.S. churchwomen, the Carter administration announced the resumption of full "lethal" military aid plus U.S. military advisers.

When President Ronald Reagan took office, the United States was solidly backing the military and the right. The new administration ratified and intensified the policy already under way, putting increased emphasis on El Salvador's alleged geopolitical importance. *Newsweek* summarized the U.S. position in March 1981:

> Washington has drawn a line in El Salvador against what it regards as the global ambitions of the Soviet Union and surrogates such as Cuba. "I believe Central America is the most important place in the world for the U.S. today," Jeane Kirkpatrick, Reagan's ambassador to the United Nations, told *Newsweek* She maintained that if the Soviets "get new beachheads, and we're talking about whole countries, they will be transformed into military bases."[17]

The Revolutionary Groups

The Communist Party (PCS) was made illegal in El Salvador after the 1932 uprising, but managed to operate politically through front groups. The PCS generally followed Moscow's advice and did not try again to promote armed rebellion; instead it concentrated on trade-union organizing and electoral politics. This strategy, plus the party's support for El Salvador's 1969 war against Honduras, led to a serious split within the left in 1970. The more radical breakaway faction formed the first of the armed guerrilla groups, the Popular Liberation Forces (FPL).

The second major guerrilla organization was the People's Revolutionary Army (ERP), created in 1971 as a result of divisions within the FPL. The ERP's founders were radical students and frustrated Christian Democrats, and they continued to criticize the PCS for clinging too long to the hope of a peaceful transition to socialism. The ERP, however, rejected the FPL's alignment with the Cuban revolution. Within five years, further internal disputes led to another split and the founding of a third guerrilla group called the Armed Forces of National Resistance (FARN). A fourth and much smaller group, the Revolutionary Party of Central American Workers (PRTC), was formed later in the decade.[18]

The official Communist Party (PCS) was the last to follow suit. The PCS had continued to rely on nonviolent organizing during the increasingly violent 1970s. It had backed the coalition for Duarte and Ungo in the ill-fated 1972 elections, and despite that experience it participated in the 1977 election as well. Not until 1980 did the PCS form a military arm, the Armed Forces of Liberation (FAL). This group and the PRTC remain the smallest of the revolutionary armed forces.

The leaders of the left naturally saw the need to coordinate their struggle, and several umbrella organizations were formed. The Farabundo Martí Front for National Liberation (FMLN) is a coalition of the five armed guerrilla groups, and it is allied with the political leadership of the Democratic Revolutionary Front (FDR). The FDR's first president was a member of an oligarchy family and former minister of agriculture, Enrique Alvarez Córdova. In the fall of 1980 Alvarez and five other members of the FDR executive committee were kidnapped and murdered by the military, operating under the cover of one of the principal right-wing death squads. At this point Guillermo Manuel Ungo, Duarte's 1972 presidential running mate, was chosen as the FDR's new leader.

In August 1981 France and Mexico jointly recognized the FDR-FMLN as a "representative political force" which should be involved in any political settlement in El Salvador. The U.S. government, by then deeply committed to military victory and opposed to any compromise, was not pleased by this suggestion. A United Nations resolution calling for a "negotiated political solution" passed the General Assembly in December 1981 only after strong U.S. objections. The FDR-FMLN leadership responded by reiterating their desire to negotiate. The United States was not interested, and any proposal for a settlement which might lead to sharing power with the revolutionary forces continues to be strongly opposed.

As the civil war drags on in the late 1980s, El Salvador's government and economy have grown ever more dependent on U.S. assistance; by the end of 1986 that assistance totalled roughly $2.5 billion. The Salvadoran army cannot win the war, but the United States is determined not to let it lose. For the people of El Salvador peace and the hope of a better life are as remote as ever.

Arming the Revolution: Is Nicaragua Responsible?

Prior to 1980, the direct involvement of outsiders in El Salvador's armed conflict was minimal. The United States had not sent arms to the Salvadoran military since 1977; on the other side, there were few claims that the guerrillas were getting significant help from foreign allies. In 1980 this picture changed. From a modest beginning that year, the United States has supplied the government of El Salvador with military equipment worth at least $600 million, while in 1980 the rebels too began receiving arms shipments from allies in Cuba and Nicaragua. The U.S. government has argued since 1981 that such foreign aid is largely responsible for the insurgency in El Salvador, but there is little factual basis for such a belief. As Napoleón Duarte stated in 1980, the real sources of revolution lie deep within the country's own history.

The military equipment of the revolutionary forces has always been vastly inferior in both quantity and sophistication to that of the government troops. Where do the guerrillas get their weapons? Here is how President Reagan addressed that question in 1983:

> I'm sure you've read about guerrillas capturing rifles from government national guard units, and recently this has happened. But much more critical to guerrilla operations are the supplies and munitions that are infiltrated into El Salvador by land, sea and air— by pack mules, by small boats, and by small aircraft. These pipelines fuel the guerrilla offensives and keep alive the conviction of their extremist leaders that power will ultimately come from the barrels of their guns.[19]

The claims that outside aid is "critical to guerrilla operations" in El Salvador, and that Nicaragua is heavily involved in supplying that aid, have been made repeatedly by the administration, which uses them to locate El Salvador's civil war within the global East/West conflict and to justify U.S. Central America policies. But are these claims true? The rest of this chapter will survey the available evidence.

A landing on the beach

On January 10, 1981, during the last weeks of the Carter administration, the Salvadoran rebels launched what they hoped would be their "final offensive." Despite initial rebel successes, government forces defeated the attempt within a few days. After the offensive had been stalemated, the United States announced that it would resume the military aid which had been suspended early in December in response to the rape and murder of the four U.S. churchwomen by soldiers. The new aid would include U.S. military advisors as well as $5 million worth of weapons and equipment.

The immediate rationale for the restoration was not the stalled offensive but reports that some 100 foreign guerrillas, plus arms and supplies, had been landed on a Salvadoran beach. U.S. ambassador Robert White was temporarily persuaded by the invasion report to reverse his opposition to renewing military assistance, and the incident was widely reported in the United States.

According to the Salvadoran government, four or five thirty-foot boats brought the invaders from Nicaragua to a coastal village named El Cuco. When reporters later visited the landing site, however, the evidence they found did not fit this story. There had been fighting in the area, but according to villagers the casualties were seven soldiers and two guerrillas killed instead of the fifty-three guerrillas claimed by the government. Other particulars were also far out of line. Lawrence Pezzullo, then the U.S. ambassador to Nicaragua, later described the boat landing story as "fictional." Ambassador White soon developed serious doubts of his own, but such second thoughts did not get the publicity given to the original invasion story and did not alter President Carter's reversal on military aid.[20]

The "white paper" of 1981

In February 1981 the State Department published a report entitled *Communist Interference in El Salvador.* Its summary claimed that the paper would present

> definitive evidence of the clandestine military support given by the Soviet Union, Cuba, and their Communist allies to Marxist-Leninist guerrillas now fighting to overthrow the established government of El Salvador. The evidence...underscores the central role played by Cuba and other Communist countries beginning in 1979 in the political unification, military direction, and arming of insurgent forces in El Salvador.[21]

The information in the white paper was said to come largely from two major caches of guerrilla documents captured by the Salvadoran government, supplemented by "evidence from other intelligence sources." Much of the paper describes Salvadoran Communist Party leader Shafik Handal's reported travels to a number of Soviet-bloc countries in search of support for the rebel forces. The paper gives specific figures, announcing that several communist states had offered to supply "nearly 800 tons of the most modern weapons and equipment," and that "nearly 200 tons of those arms" had reached El Salvador, "mostly through Cuba and Nicaragua." Its conclusion has been much quoted:

In short, over the past year, the insurgency in El Salvador has been progressively transformed into a textbook case of indirect armed aggression by Communist powers through Cuba.

The white paper served as political propaganda to advance administration policy, but it did not stand up when subjected to informed criticism. The paper's distortions of history and faulty political analysis were underlined by several analysts soon after its publication.[22] Among others, Phillip Berryman of the American Friends Service Committee pointed out some of its major errors: lack of historical perspective; exaggeration of the role of the Salvadoran Communist Party (PCS), in reality one of the less important groups in the FMLN; the pretense that the Salvadoran government was a progressive force for reform, attacked from both left and right; failure to mention the major role of the popular organizations; false assertions that the left was without popular support; and more.

Subsequent investigations exposed faulty methodology and fraud in the research and writing of the white paper. A June 1981 article in the *Wall Street Journal* quoted the paper's principal author, Jon Glassman of the State Department, as admitting that parts of it were "misleading" and "over-embellished," and that its preparation involved "mistakes" and "guessing." Reporters from the *Journal* and the *Washington Post* examined many of the documents on which the white paper was based, and found that they simply did not back up the paper's claims. Several of the documents were attributed to people who didn't write them; the real authors were often unknown. Statistics were "extrapolated." The *Post* commented that "In one key document the State Department dropped a sentence from its translation into English, which undermines the Department's characterization of the document." And according to the *Journal*, "Much information in the white paper can't be found in the documents at all."[23]

The "200 tons" of military supplies said to have reached the guerrillas is one such piece of non-information in the white paper; none of the documents mention any such figure. According to Glassman, it was "extrapolated" on the basis of "other intelligence," but the *Journal* found the other intelligence unconvincing. The "nearly 800 tons" of promised equipment was also an "extrapolation."

Most important is that many of the documents point to conclusions opposite to those reached in the white paper. Instead of a revolutionary force lavishly supplied with arms from communist countries, they show that the guerrilla groups faced serious shortages and difficulties with supply. According to the *Post*, "In document after document there are reports of rebels short of arms, or looking for ways to buy arms, or exhorting comrades to produce home-made arms, or plotting to kidnap wealthy Salvadorans thought to have access to private arsenals." As these press reports belatedly made clear, the conclusions of the white paper were unsupported by the evidence, and were even to some extent contradicted by it. The administration's manipulation of the facts casts doubt on the existence of any major arms flow to the revolutionaries in El Salvador, since if the flow were actually happening, genuine evidence should have been easy to produce.

What weapons do the guerrillas have?

Many outside observers have visited the rebel forces in different parts of El Salvador. Dr. Charles Clements lived and worked in the rebel-controlled Guazapa zone during 1982 and 1983. Clements recalls an evening in March 1982; an attack was planned to take place the next day:

> Around me, the guerrillas looked to their sorry store of weapons, cleaning and recleaning them and checking their ammunition. When they went to battle the next day they would be armed with U.S. M-16s, Belgian FALs, German G-3s, plus a few old M-1s and .30 calibre carbines. With the exception of a rusty Chinese RPG II grenade launcher—the only non-western weapon I would see all year—there were no heavier weapons among them.[24]

Clements's testimony about military matters is credible; before becoming a doctor and a pacifist he was an honor graduate of the U.S. Air Force Academy and flew over fifty combat missions as a pilot in Vietnam. He writes, "I kept looking for evidence of Cuban or Nicaraguan or even Soviet advisors among the insurgents, certain that there must be at least a few." But he found none at all. On one occasion villagers who heard his accented Spanish asked Clements whether he was himself a Russian. He explains that "They had heard the phrase 'Soviet-backed' insurgency on Voice of America so many times that they assumed it was true."[25]

Clements tells of meeting a few foreigners serving with the revolution—a Mexican, an Argentine and a Colombian—but no Nicaraguans, Cubans or Russians. He recalls how Raul Hércules, the leader of guerrilla military operations in Guazapa, and other rebels were insulted at the implication that they had not made the revolution themselves:

We don't need Cubans and we don't need Nicaraguans. And we don't need the *norteamericanos.* This is an authentic revolution, as yours was. We know what we're fighting for....

You *norteamericanos* will not control our country, and neither will the Soviets. If we must fight to victory, we will. It is only a matter of time.[26]

A number of journalists have also visited rebel-held areas in El Salvador and observed the guerrilla forces. Some of these experiences are summarized by Raymond Bonner, who agrees with Charlie Clements: no Russians, Cubans or Nicaraguans have been observed serving with the revolutionary forces, and the guerrillas' weapons show little evidence of significant arms support from outside.[27]

But journalists and other outsiders have seen guerrillas returning from raids heavily loaded with equipment captured from the Salvadoran army. In addition, the rebels' humane treatment of prisoners has encouraged government soldiers, often unenthusiastic conscripts, to surrender. Prisoners have usually been released, but their weapons and equipment remain in rebel hands. The FMLN claims that most of its weapons are obtained in this way, and several Reagan administration officials told the *New York Times* nearly the same thing in 1983.[28] In addition to captures, members of the government forces sometimes sell U.S.-supplied weapons to the revolutionary forces (as happened frequently in Vietnam).

Former Lt. Colonel Edward King is another witness with military credentials. He writes that

> There is little public evidence to support the Administration's claim that arms continue to be shipped from points in Nicaragua to El Salvador for the Farabundo Martí Liberation Front (FMLN), the Salvadoran rebel forces.
>
> Visits to FMLN units reveal that those units are critically short of crew-served direct fire weapons and anti-aircraft weapons—all of which are readily available in Nicaragua. But none of those weapons have been sent to the FMLN, which is forced to attack chiefly with rifles, machine guns and captured U.S. mortars and 90mm guns. And FMLN units are short of ammunition for the variety of weapons they use: not an indication of a source of steady supply.[29]

The 1983 and 1984 Background Papers

In May 1983 and July 1984 the State and Defense Departments published "Background Papers" continuing the exposition of the Cuban-Nicaraguan threat begun with the 1981 white paper.[30] The 1983 paper reports diplomatic contacts and radio or press statements by leftist leaders, plus allegations of arms shipments and claims of insight into Cuban strategic thinking. Statements attributed to captured guerrilla officers and other prisoners are used to "prove" the complicity of Nicaragua and Cuba in arms transports to El Salvador, criminal activity in Costa Rica, and other Central American unrest. The paper contains no documents and makes many unsupported allegations—for example, it offers a map of Central America on which broad multicolored arrows point vaguely from Nicaragua toward El Salvador to display "the known major infiltration routes" for arms smuggling. The 1983 paper also repeats some of the claims of the 1981 white paper, including both the figures (200 tons for weapons shipped to El Salvador and 800 tons for weapons promised to El Salvador) which the author of the 1981 paper admitted were without foundation.

The 1984 paper contains more new material, although it too reprises dubious "extrapolations" from its discredited predecessor. The paper describes and exaggerates Nicaragua's military buildup, and asserts that since 1981 "there has been a steady flow of ammunition, explosives, medicines and clothing" to revolutionary forces in El Salvador. There are also some new specifics:

> Vessels disguised as fishing boats leave from Nicaragua's northwestern coast and then transfer arms to large motorized canoes which ply the myriad bays and inlets of El Salvador's southeast coast. Two active Nicaraguan transshipment points for delivery of military supplies to Salvadoran guerrillas were attacked and damaged by anti-Sandinista forces in September 1983. These were located at La Concha in Estero de Padre Ramos, 40 km NW of Corinto, and at Potosi on the Gulf of Fonseca.[31]

Edward King visited one of these "active transshipment points" in May 1984, shortly before the publication of the State-Defense paper alleging arms smuggling there. King describes Potosi as "a tiny village at the tip of a Nicaraguan peninsula extending out into the Gulf of Fonseca." He reports that "there is only one narrow, muddy, rutted road from Potosi to the beach area" from which arms are said to be shipped. A building described in the *Background Paper* as a "warehouse" was abandoned, as were several sheds noted in the government's aerial photograph. King's report continues:

> There was neither a road suitable for truck traffic nor any sign of passage of vehicles carrying heavy cargo to a debarkation point....There was no evidence of the normal residue found at an unloading and loading site. Indeed, the surrounding area appeared uninhabited. The main road into the Potosi port area is overgrown with grass and weeds, not a sign that cargo-bearing vehicles had passed through recently....
>
> During much of 1983 and 1984, the U.S. operated a radar station on Tiger Island in the Gulf of Fonseca and stationed a radar-equipped frigate at the mouth of the Gulf. Over a period of approximately 10 months this extreme surveillance did not reveal a pattern of systematic night-time supply to El Salvador from Potosi.[32]

The August 1984 News Briefing

Government spokespeople sometimes assert that "classified intelligence information" would prove their case if only they were free to reveal it. In the summer of 1984 State Department officials gave classified briefings to members of Congress which they said offered evidence of the supply of weapons to Salvadoran rebels from Cuba and Nicaragua. Finally they presented "about 95 percent of the key information in the briefing" at a public press conference, and the result was published as a booklet.[33]

The briefing described the alleged infiltration of weapons by sea. It reported that the Salvadoran army had captured maps in skirmishes with guerrilla units. The maps, displayed at the briefing, show supply routes within El Salvador which lead inland from the coast. Also on display were photos of radar screens aboard U.S. AC-130 aircraft which "can see in the nighttime" and which fly frequent reconnaissance flights over southeastern El Salvador. The radar was said to show large fishing boats meeting offshore with much smaller boats. The small boats then approached the coast and apparently unloaded something on the beach which was carried inland by people using pack animals. Finally, one of the large boats moved away "in a southwesterly direction towards open seas." The origin and destination of the large boats are not mentioned.

Former CIA analyst David MacMichael has commented on this evidence:

The point of all this was to implicate Nicaragua. So at last we've had an intelligence breakthrough! We have taken one of these arms ships under surveillance, and of course we're going to maintain this surveillance until we track it back to its base, right? And if that base is Nicaragua, that is going to be the feature of the presentation. The feature is not the arms going across the beach, it is this trawler going back to Potosi or Puerto Sandino or Corinto or someplace else.

Well, there is no mention of Nicaragua, none whatsoever! What can this mean? Assuming the trawler was kept under surveillance, it must mean it went somewhere else. And if it wasn't kept under surveillance somebody should be courtmartialed. What a fiasco![34]

In the briefing General Paul Gorman, head of the U.S. Southern Command, also described land infiltration routes from Honduras. Again there is no indication that the weapons which may have been brought into El Salvador came from Nicaraguan territory, much less that the Nicaraguan government was responsible for shipping them. Gorman noted that a number of U.S.-made rifles captured from the guerrillas were identified through their serial numbers as weapons used in Vietnam, rather than weapons supplied to the Salvadoran army. Col. Ed King discussed this point:

> It is plausible that some of the M-16s captured by North Vietnam were shipped to Russia, then to Cuba and eventually to Nicaragua. But it is equally possible that the North Vietnamese sold large numbers of their estimated 100,000 or more captured M-16s to international arms merchants in return for desperately needed foreign exchange. These gun runners may have then sold the rifles to the FMLN.[35]

If the material made public in this briefing is typical of the classified information in the U.S. government's possession, the allegation of a major arms flow from Nicaragua to El Salvador would remain unproven even in case all such secrets were revealed.

What the CIA knows: an insider's testimony

A former CIA intelligence analyst, David MacMichael, has provided an inside look at what the U.S. government really knows about the arms traffic; this section is based on an interview with him in November 1985. MacMichael began working for the CIA in 1981 with an extensive background in Latin America, the Far East, and military intelligence.[36] At the CIA he became an "estimates officer," one of fif-

teen or sixteen analysts working in support of the National Intelligence Council. In the fall of 1981 MacMichael learned about the CIA's plan to organize a military force made up of former Somoza National Guardsmen. He took his superiors seriously when they explained that the purpose was to interdict the arms flow from Nicaragua to El Salvador. MacMichael had experience with guerrilla organization in South Vietnam, and he immediately asked to see the "prior analysis" of the supply system which the FMLN forces used. He discovered, he says, that

> It had never been done. So I began to look into that, and then I started looking seriously at the question of the so-called arms flow. It was readily apparent right away that there was no arms flow going on. Oh sure, there had been the period of the famous and ill-fated Salvadoran guerrilla general offensive in January 1981 with which they hoped to present a fait accompli to the new U.S. administration. At that time the Nicaraguans, along with the Panamanians, Costa Ricans and many others, had been involved in delivery of arms and other material support to the FMLN.

> When the Reagan administration came in, there was clear evidence that arms were going from Nicaragua to El Salvador, either with the cooperation of the Nicaraguan government at some level or at least without effective action at the top levels to stop it. This was roughly November 1980 to perhaps as late as March 1981. That evidence was immediately used to cut off the U.S. assistance to Nicaragua and to issue very strong warnings that very bad things would happen to them if they continued this practice.

> It is at this point that the arms-flow evidence simply disappears. That's interesting from an intelligence point of view, because we had had evidence over a period of time of all the sort of things that you expect to happen if there is a flow: a truck is captured, an airplane crashes....Then it stopped.

MacMichael's assertion that Nicaraguan supplies to the FMLN ended in early 1981 was confirmed by the U.S. State Department at the time. On April 1, 1981 the Department announced that U.S. aid to Nicaragua, suspended since January, was being cancelled. The *New York Times* reported:

> Paradoxically, the decision to terminate the remaining $15 million in aid came as the State Department said that in the last few weeks Nicaragua had virtually halted all flow of arms from its territory to insurgents in El Salvador.

A State Department spokesman said that the Reagan administration had made "strong representations" to Nicaragua to halt the flow, and that

> Their response has been positive. We have no hard evidence of arms movements through Nicaragua during the past few weeks, and propaganda and some other support activities have been curtailed.[37]

The spokesman added that the administration was considering a resumption of Food for Peace aid "if the favorable trends continue there." According to MacMichael the "favorable trends"—the halt to the arms flow—did continue, but the administration did not resume aid to Nicaragua. Instead, it prepared to expand the CIA's covert activities, already begun in March 1981, into the contra war. When the administration told Congress about these plans in December, it explained they were necessary to interdict the (now mostly non-existent) flow of weapons and supplies to the Salvadoran revolutionaries.[38]

MacMichael said that Larry Eagleburger, then assistant secretary of state for European affairs, together with a high-ranking CIA officer, used the February 1981 white paper to promote the U.S. case:

> They formed a team that went zipping off to Europe directly after the new administration came in....
>
> The basic strategy was to define the situation in Central America as a direct and dangerous Soviet challenge. You would publicly identify it as such. Then you would move with resolve and dispatch to face that challenge, knowing it wasn't a real challenge at all, and emerge in a very short period with a resounding "victory." This would serve all sorts of domestic and foreign political purposes for the new Reagan administration....That was the purpose of the famous white paper. One is entitled to suspect this whole operation.

MacMichael stressed the political role of the alleged arms flow from Nicaragua:

> It's important for people to understand how central this business of the so-called arms flow has been to the whole policy pattern. You have to go back to 1979 when the pressures were coming on the Carter administration. Very strong elements within the Department of State and in the intelligence organizations had been violently opposed to the Panama Canal Treaty and to the whole approach to policy in the region, where the United States tradi-

tion is absolute, hegemonic and unilateral control. The idea of sharing control of the Canal Zone with Panama, the idea of bringing in Mexico and Venezuela as regional secondary powers which had direct interests—this flies in the face of a hundred years of tradition and practice in the Department of State, and that sort of momentum is not easily changed.

So the pressure was on Mr. White [U.S. Ambassador to El Salvador] to approve a renewal of arms aid. Archbishop Romero had pleaded with him publicly not to. What was needed to change Mr. White's thinking?

It was the discovery of an "arms shipment" on the beach near La Unión. I believe that was a plant. It was so clumsy, so ridiculous— little trails of grenades leading into the underbrush like in Hansel and Gretel! But it was enough, briefly, for Mr. White to bow to the pressure and say "Yes, this shows there is an aggression here, a Nicaraguan intervention." This took place in January 1981, just before the Reagan administration.

The point I'm making is that arms is the key element. This has been used as the legitimating device throughout.

MacMichael also comments on the *Background Paper* of July 1984, explaining that members of Congress received an advance copy of the paper in late June:

I had already gone public with my charge about the lack of evidence for this arms flow. So I was surprised and even delighted to see that the specific paragraph dealing with this matter of the arms flow said essentially that there was no arms flow, but there were sporadic deliveries of ammunition, medicines and clothing coming from Nicaragua. The point is that the former claim of a continuing flood, a massive flow of arms, had been abandoned! I pointed that out to the *New York Times* and some other people, and it went out on the wire. The next thing you know this advance copy was being declared a *draft*, and on July 19 a new paper was issued which restored the charge of a continuing, massive flood of arms.

The State Department in 1985 published still another document attempting to prove its case against Nicaragua on the arms flow.[39] MacMichael called this paper "the most mendacious document of all time" because it uses deliberate deception right on the cover: the title of the paper, *Revolution Beyond Our Borders,* is taken from a speech by Nicaraguan Interior Minister Tomás Borge, but he is quoted out of con-

text in a manner which suggests the opposite of what he actually said.[40] In this paper, MacMichael says, "they have abandoned practically all the old proofs," and adds that the paper relies heavily on the statements of a "defected and/or captured" FMLN officer, Napoleón Romero. MacMichael had several comments on this testimony:

> Romero states that he is the man responsible for the supply of one of the major branches of the FMLN, the FPL, which has about three thousand fighters. It's very interesting that he talks about receiving supplies by air up until about February 1981. And he talks about a plane that crashed—and that did happen—back in January or December. And then there were no more supplies that came by air. This is interesting because it directly contradicts the statements, that have been made by the Department of State over the past four years, that these air supplies went on. But they didn't seem to notice this.

> This guy [Romero] tells that he was handling 20,000 to 30,000 rounds of ammunition per month. That's how many rounds per guerrilla? Six to eight, ten at most. *This* is the massive flow of arms? The Department goes on to point out that this amount of ammunition, packed into fifty metal cans, would weigh about 1,340 pounds, and this could be man-packed by about eighteen people, or put on six pack animals, or into one small pickup truck. And this is what they are reduced to by their own testimony! This massive flow of arms is something you could run out of your aunt's garage—and it may well *be* run out of your aunt's garage for all I know. This is the reductio ad absurdum!

MacMichael said there was no convincing evidence about the source of this ammunition, adding,

> Of course Napoleón Romero is saying that it's coming from Nicaragua. And he could be right; I can't directly impeach anybody—except to give you the common-sense dictum of intelligence analysis that the least reliable source is the defector. The very least reliable—because he's got to sell himself as well as anything else.

The World Court Ruling

When the CIA mined Nicaraguan harbors in 1984, the Nicaraguan government appealed to the International Court of Justice in The Hague (the World Court) and charged the United States with aggression. In May 1984 the court issued a preliminary order requiring the United States to stop these attacks and to respect Nicaraguan sovereignty. The

Reagan administration argued that its actions against Nicaragua were legally and morally justified as "defense" against Nicaragua's "armed attack" on El Salvador; it was Nicaragua's alleged role in supplying weapons to the Salvadoran revolutionaries which supposedly constituted the attack. In effect, however, the administration admitted the weakness of its case by withdrawing from the court's proceedings in November 1984.

David MacMichael scoffed at the claim that the United States had convincing evidence which it couldn't present in public because its intelligence sources must be protected:

> In the case of the World Court, the administration had the opportunity to blow the Nicaraguans completely out of the park, if they could prove their case about the arms flow. What are they saving their "sources and methods" for, the Junior Prom? I know this stuff very well, and it's crazy. We have already exposed all the sources and methods we could possibly use.

> This business is strange. We publish the pictures that we take from illegal overflights of Nicaraguan territory; we don't care about that. We publish the types of radar that we use for surveillance. You can go right to *Jane's* and look it up and see what the attributes of these radars are.[41] You might assume that they are protecting cryptographic methods, but those no longer count. That's World War II stuff.

> The other thing is that you don't want to expose an agent. My answer to this is that if the agents are any good, why haven't there been any results from their information in over four years? Why haven't they seized the odd arms shipment or two just to test whether the information is any good? And they haven't seized any.

On June 27, 1986 the World Court issued its ruling in Nicaragua's suit against the United States. Although the U.S. government did not present witnesses, the court examined U.S. documents such as *Revolution Beyond Our Borders* plus material and arguments submitted before the United States withdrew. The decision was that U.S. actions against Nicaragua since 1981 are in violation of international law. The claim that the United States is acting in "collective self-defense" together with Nicaragua's neighbors was rejected both as a matter of law and because it lacked a factual basis. The court did find that "between July 1979...and the early months of 1981, an intermittent flow of arms was routed via the territory of Nicaragua to the armed opposition in El Salvador." But the judgement went on to state:

The Court was not, however, satisfied that assistance has reached the Salvadoran armed opposition, on a scale of any significance, since the early months of 1981, or that the Government of Nicaragua was responsible for the flow of arms at either period.[42]

*   *   *

U.S. allegations of a continuing, major flow of weapons from Cuba through Nicaragua to the Salvadoran revolutionaries have been an important tool which the Reagan administration has used to increase congressional support for its war efforts in both Nicaragua and El Salvador. The arms-flow claims provided the first rationale for U.S. sponsorship of the contra forces. But, as the World Court's decision underscores, the evidence to support the charges is not there. Nicaragua provides the FMLN with political support and sympathy, but little of a material nature. El Salvador's bloody conflict remains a civil war, whose causes lie in the injustice and repression long characteristic of Salvadoran society. The one outside power heavily involved in the war, supplying massive economic and military support to the side it favors, is the United States.

5

Needed: A New Approach

> We surely can not deny to any nation that right whereon our own
> government is founded—that every one may govern itself accord-
> ing to its own will, and that it may transact its business through
> whatever organ it thinks proper, whether king, convention, as-
> sembly, committee, president or anything else it may choose.

> —Thomas Jefferson

"The Communists Are Out to Get Us"

The U.S. approach to Central America has multiple motives, which
jointly produce one clear result: an inordinate fear of social unrest and
revolution. Policymakers evidently believe that substantial social
change may diminish or end the long-established pattern of U.S.
domination. This fear of losing control is often stated in terms of a need
to defend the region from Soviet or Cuban influence. It is not politically palatable in the United States to speak openly of denying the right
of self-determination to other countries; it is much more acceptable to
"defend against communist takeovers."

President Reagan states the challenge to U.S. interests this way:

> Central America has become the stage for a bold attempt by the
> Soviet Union, Cuba, and Nicaragua to install communism, by force,
> throughout this hemisphere.[1]

He describes this threat as extending even to the United States itself:

71

> The national security of all the Americas is at stake in Central
> America. If we cannot defend ourselves there...the safety of our
> homeland would be put in jeopardy.[2]

The administration asserts that "communist subversion" is "spreading
southward and northward" and creates "the threat that 100 million
people from Panama to the open border on our south could come
under the control of pro-Soviet regimes."[3]

No pains have been spared in trying to communicate this fearful
vision to the American public. In an unusually frank comment, Deputy
Assistant Secretary of the Air Force J. Michael Kelly asserted:

> I think the most critical special operations mission we have today
> is to persuade the American people that the communists are out
> to get us.[4]

The purpose of that "mission" is to justify the continuing massive U.S.
military intervention in Central America, and to prepare the way for interventions in other parts of the Third World as well.

This study has examined the reality of alleged Soviet and/or communist threats in Central America. There is a crisis of major proportions
in the region, and the effects are tragic for the people who live there.
But the situation does not resemble the fearful picture drawn by the
U.S. government, which persists in describing Central American conflicts as part of the global East/West rivalry. In reality, the roots of the
Central American crisis lie within the region, in long-established poverty and oppression. Revolution is a response to this history of injustice.
The real danger is that local conflicts may be engulfed in regional war
if the United States continues investing its prestige and power to ensure that fundamental social change does not take place. Alternative
policies could serve both U.S. and Central American needs far better
than the present attempt to rely on military power in order to maintain
U.S. control.

U.S. Goals: The Rhetoric
and the Reality

Administration officials usually describe U.S. foreign policy aims
in terms of lofty principles. Secretary of State George Shultz, for ex-

ample, says that U.S. objectives are "to prevent a wider crisis and to bring about a lasting peace":

> And to achieve those ends, the President defined four activities to which we have committed ourselves: support for democracy, reform, and human rights; support for economic development; support for dialogue and negotiations among the countries of the region and within each country; and support for the security of the region's threatened nations as a shield for democratization, development and diplomacy.[5]

This sounds fine. But the real intentions of any government can not be learned from such statements of principles; instead, they must be inferred by watching what that government actually does. The actions of the United States in Central America, past and present, are clearly inconsistent with the goals stated by Mr. Shultz.

The U.S. government says that human rights and democracy are its concern, but the United States has consistently backed regimes which trample upon those values. The Reagan administration claims to want more democracy and less militarism in Nicaragua, but it pressures Nicaragua in the opposite direction by undermining its economy, attempting to subvert its elections, and above all by sponsoring a bloody "covert" war while U.S. troops constantly maneuver just across the Honduran border. The United States holds up Costa Rican democracy as a model, but it is seriously undermining the peace and welfare of that nation as well, by pushing it toward conflict with Nicaragua. Washington pays lip service to international law while it rejects the authority and judgement of the World Court. If peace and democracy are really U.S. goals in Central America, these policies are counterproductive.

Nothing shows the disparity between professed ideals and reality more clearly than the methods which the Reagan administration has employed against Nicaragua.[6] Its campaign includes economic and credit boycotts, shelling and mining of Nicaragua's harbors by the CIA and repeated threats of invasion, but the centerpiece is U.S. promotion of the contra war. The contra forces are not an uprising of the Nicaraguan people; they were organized by outsiders from the remnants of former dictator Somoza's National Guard. The main target of contra attacks has been Nicaragua's civilian society. According to Americas Watch, the contras have "routinely attacked civilian populations. Their forces kidnap, torture, and murder health workers, teachers, and other government employees." Many other observers report similar

findings.[7] Such conduct exactly fits this definition by the U.S. State
Department:

> *Terrorism* is premeditated, politically motivated violence per-
> petrated against noncombatant targets by subnational groups or
> clandestine state agents.[8]

Although President Reagan calls the contras "freedom fighters" and the
"moral equal" of the U.S. founding fathers, by the standards which the
United States uses elsewhere they are more accurately described as
murderers and terrorists.

Copyright 1985 Tony Auth. Reprinted with permission.

Implementing the vendetta against Nicaragua has been harmful
to openness and democracy within the United States. The majority of
U.S. citizens have opposed the contra war since the public first learned
of its existence; polls taken during 1986 give the same result.[9] Moreover,
since late 1986 the press and (in 1987) congressional hearings have
revealed that U.S. government officials financed and promoted the war
against Nicaragua using bizarre methods of doubtful legality, methods
kept secret from Congress and the public alike. The use of such tactics, and the disregard of public and congressional opposition, casts
doubt on the Reagan administration's dedication to democratic principles at home as well as abroad. The president has in effect claimed
the right to act outside and above the requirements of domestic and in-

ternational law. If tolerated, these actions threaten to subvert the U.S. constitution and the rule of law, in the name of national security and anti-communism.

The anti-Nicaragua campaign has also isolated the United States internationally and damaged its credibility. The policy has failed to gain approval from any important U.S. allies in Europe or Latin America.[10] As Vermont Senator Patrick Leahy reported,

> All our allies in the region, including those comprising the Contadora nations and the Contadora support groups, have publicly called on the President to cease aid to the contras....Our government is in the strange situation of officially and piously endorsing the Contadora peace process, while simultaneously ignoring the pleas of the very countries who are looking for a diplomatic settlement that would stop the fighting and reduce regional tensions.[11]

The Case of Honduras

U.S. policy in Honduras offers a different but equally clear illustration of the contradictions between rhetoric and reality. During the 1980s Honduras has become an essential U.S. base of operations in Central America. It is the primary staging area for the contra war against Nicaragua, and plays an important role in U.S. efforts to defeat the Salvadoran revolution. In support of these objectives, the United States provided Honduras with over one billion dollars in aid between 1982 and 1987 and has sponsored a major military buildup there. U.S. armed forces have conducted maneuvers in Honduras almost continuously since mid-1983, often jointly with the Honduran army. As the country has been militarized, its national budget has become dependent on U.S. aid, producing powerful pressure on the Honduran government to give the United States whatever military and political support it asks.[12]

The impact on Honduras itself has been heavy. Most of the Yankee dollars have gone, directly or indirectly, into the military buildup, and have done little to feed malnourished children or create jobs for their unemployed parents.[13] (Some 60 percent of the workforce lacks full-time employment.) U.S. aid to the Honduran armed forces has strengthened their already great power in national politics; lack of civilian control over the military is a major obstacle to real democracy. As is sadly predictable, towns in the vicinity of U.S. bases have seen an explosive rise in prostitution, which has been called the "growth industry" for women in the military buildup. During the buildup political killings increased sharply, while "disappearances" began to occur in Honduras for the first time.

The thousands of heavily-armed contras, with their military leadership in Tegucigalpa and their bases near the Nicaraguan border, pose difficult problems for Honduras. Their presence and activities create a constant danger of war between the two countries, a war neither country wants. Human rights activists have evidence that contras were involved in many of the political murders of the 1980s.[14] Farmers complain that their livelihoods are being destroyed as contras increase their control over land, towns and roads in southern Honduras. Even high government officials worry about what will happen if the contras lose hope of gaining a victory in Nicaragua and make their presence permanent. A delegation of members of the Honduran Congress visited Washington in May 1986 to ask that the contras be removed from Honduras, and that the $100 million slated for them be given instead to the Contadora group of nations for peaceful purposes.[15]

The militarization sponsored by the United States has brought many Hondurans to feel they are living in an occupied country. Dr. Ramón Custodio, president of the Honduran Committee for the Defense of Human Rights, describes the situation this way:

> Currently the foreign policy of Honduras has been totally subordinated to the interests of the United States. The presence of a foreign army in the form of U.S. troops...and the armed groups of Somocistas on the border financed by the CIA in order to attack Nicaragua, all this shows what a sad role Honduras has come to play in the history of intervention against its neighbors.[16]

What Does the United States Want?

These examples indicate that what U.S. policymakers say about democracy, human rights and human welfare is not the real basis for U.S. strategy toward Central America. Maintaining U.S. dominance in the region is the bottom line. Analyst and author Phillip Berryman put it this way: "What is the United States up to in Central America? 'Stopping revolution' would seem to be a coherent and comprehensive answer."[17]

Why is "stopping revolution" essential? Above all, because the U.S. government regards Central America as one small battlefield in the global U.S./Soviet competition for supremacy. Radical social change, gains in power by popular mass movements or the political left, strivings for economic independence and non-alignment internationally—all these must be opposed, for they threaten U.S. control and so are equated to gains for the Soviet adversary. U.S. actions based on such beliefs have had tragic consequences for the people of the region, whose lives and concerns count for little in U.S. eyes by comparison with the larger issues supposedly at stake there. In its struggle against the "evil empire," the U.S. government can sacrifice human rights and still believe it is engaged in a righteous fight.

It would be misleading, however, to attribute current U.S. policy in Central America entirely to anti-communism and fear of Soviet influence. U.S. intervention in the region is not new; the United States has exercised control over Central America since the middle of the nineteenth century in all matters it regards as affecting U.S. interests. The control was often exerted through non-military pressures, but force was used whenever it was thought necessary. As the 1910 Nicaraguan adventures of Marine Corps General Smedley Butler underline, the drive for hegemony predates the existence of the Soviet Union. No one fantasized in those days about communist challenges to U.S. security; dangers to U.S. commercial interests were quite sufficient to justify military intervention.

Administrations long preceding Ronald Reagan's have regarded Central America as belonging within the United States' sphere of influence. That belief was clearly stated by Undersecretary of State Robert Olds in a 1927 "Confidential Memorandum on the Nicaraguan Situation":

> International practice over a long period of time has enforced the idea of a dominant influence by this country in Central American affairs. Our ministers accredited to the five little republics stretching from the Mexican border to Panama have always been more than mere diplomatic representatives. They have been advisers whose advice has been accepted virtually as law in the capitals where they respectively reside...Call it a sphere of influence, or what you will, we do control the destinies of Central America, and we do so for the simple reason that the national interest absolutely dictates such a course.[18]

That kind of control is no longer possible. Even in Olds's time U.S. military intervention was not an unqualified success; in Nicaragua it led to seven years of fighting against the resistance headed by Augusto César Sandino. The rise and survival of nationalist movements in the region, of peoples and countries asserting their independence, is a trend that cannot be reversed. But this has been a bitter pill for U.S. leaders to swallow.

Every U.S. administration since the 1950s has fought against the loss of hegemony in the Western Hemisphere, and every administration has played on the fear of communism in designing policies to maintain or restore control. There have been "successes," such as the CIA's overthrow of Guatemala's democratic government in 1954, the invasion of the Dominican Republic in 1965, and the occupation of Grenada in 1983. But in a larger sense these policies have failed, for the movement toward self-determination has continued to grow.

What Should the United States Do?

Current U.S. policy toward Central America is a costly failure. Fear is at the bottom of this policy—not fear of Nicaraguan tanks or Salvadoran guerrillas, but fear of weakening U.S. control in a region successive administrations have identified as "our backyard." It is true that when the Nicaraguan people overthrew the Somoza regime in 1979, the ability of the United States to order events suffered a setback. But only if the world is viewed as a zero-sum game must Nicaragua's move toward independence and non-alignment be interpreted as a Soviet gain and a U.S. defeat.

There is fear that the weakening of U.S. control may prove contagious. Might the Nicaraguan revolution, left free to develop, produce a dangerous example—an example, that is, of a successful transformation from an unjust, backward society into one with far greater benefits for the majority of its citizens? Such a possibility might prove alluring to oppressed people elsewhere. The hypothesis that the United States above all fears the idea of a successful revolution goes far to explain this country's actions.

The basis for a more courageous and compassionate approach to Central America is not hard to find once the East/West paradigm and the fear of social change are put aside. In its ideals of freedom and democracy, the United States has offered the world much to admire. Is it not conceivable that a foreign policy could be developed which is truly consistent with those ideals?[19] Several points will be basic when a future U.S. administration attempts to chart such a course:

1. *Keeping Central America free of nuclear weapons and support systems* is the primary U.S. national security concern in the region.

The United States is threatened today, as it has been for decades, by the possibility of nuclear war. Stopping the nuclear arms race and moving toward mutual U.S./Soviet nuclear disarmament should be an urgent priority for U.S. foreign policy. Measures toward this goal, such as the treaty signed in December 1987 to eliminate intermediate-range nuclear missiles, are the best way to advance U.S. security. Further steps in this direction, including a comprehensive ban on nuclear weapons tests, cuts in nuclear arsenals and a halt to the development of new missiles, are essential as well.

Assuring the nuclear weapon-free status of Central America is a legitimate and important U.S. national security concern. This objective can be achieved through diplomacy better than through seeking control of the region. All the Central American nations have ratified the Treaty for the Prohibition of Nuclear Weapons in Latin America. The United States should join with other nations to monitor and maintain compliance with that treaty, and it should demonstrate its own full compliance by proving that no U.S. nuclear weapons are based in or controlled from Puerto Rico or the U.S. base in Guantanamo, Cuba. Efforts should then be made to persuade all Latin American nations not now participating to join the nuclear-free zone.

2. *The United States should proceed to normalize its relations with Cuba,* both by establishing diplomatic relations and by resuming normal trade.

Peace and stability in the Americas could only gain through improved U.S./Cuban relations, and Cuba has several times indicated a willingness to begin such negotiations. Cuba's relationship with the Soviet Union and its military presence in Africa are the stated reasons for the continued U.S. refusal to normalize relations, but refusal does nothing to alter these policies; it may instead reinforce them, especially the first. The United States must acknowledge that Cuba has compelling historical grounds for fearing U.S. threats to its security, and should seek ways to assure Cuba that it will not be so threatened in the future. Success could eventually reduce Cuba's dependence on the military support of the USSR, and would also remove obstacles to Cuba's adherence to the Treaty of Tlatelolco, both of which are desirable goals for U.S. diplomacy.

3. *Peace must be a U.S. priority.* As a step toward peace, the United States should halt its own warlike activity in the region.

This must include ending all U.S. support for the contras, ending military maneuvers and construction in Honduras, and halting U.S. participation in El Salvador's civil war. It should also include stopping all forms of economic warfare against Nicaragua and re-establishing normal trade relations. The United States has nothing to fear from any of the small nations of Central America, and would run no risk by relaxing its domination. If social conflicts in the region lead to additional revolutionary movements taking power, the United States should not deny them the acceptance which it has in the past freely offered to many military governments that have seized power through coups. The United States should seek the withdrawal of any foreign military presence at the same time it removes its own; such mutual disengagement appears to be readily attainable. (See point five below.)

Militarism has been a curse to the people of Central America. Over the years, the military establishments of the region have had very little to do with defense against outside attack, and a great deal to do with repression of their own populations and the preservation by force of unjust social orders. Costa Rica has illustrated the benefits which may be gained by limiting the military sector. The United States should work to reduce militarism throughout the region. This includes stopping direct and indirect U.S. military aid and arms sales there, and attempting to persuade other nations to do likewise.

4. *The United States should respect international law* and live up to its treaty commitments, including the United Nations Charter and that of the Organization of American States (OAS).

The United States should accept the judgement of the World Court that its attack on Nicaragua is illegal, and should carry out its obligations under that judgement. In the future, this country should attempt to strengthen rather than to undermine the court's role. U.S. adherence to the UN and OAS Charters explicitly rules out the "option" of military intervention in another nation, such as the invasion of Grenada in 1983.

5. *The security of Central America should be assured through regional agreements* like the proposed Contadora treaty, and through international institutions.

The Contadora process has been the most promising mechanism for moving toward regional peace; in 1987 it was supplemented by the proposals of Costa Rican President Oscar Arias which led to the process, but it has maneuvered to block agreements and to prevent the achievement of peace.

The four nations of the Contadora group (Mexico, Venezuela, Panama and Colombia) began their work toward a solution to regional conflicts in January 1983. In the summer of 1984 a proposed treaty was developed, and on September 7 it went to the presidents of the five Central American nations for signature. The United States called the draft "much improved" over earlier versions and said it strongly backed the negotiations. U.S. officials were reportedly confident that Nicaragua would not accept the proposed treaty.[20]

But Nicaragua did accept, offering major concessions to meet U.S. concerns. The result in Washington was not joy but dismay, and U.S. diplomats quickly set to work to make sure the treaty would not go into effect. The *Washington Post* reported these efforts in a story entitled "U.S. Urges Allies to Reject Contadora Plan." According to the *Post*,

> The United States is urging its allies in Central America to reject a regional peace treaty as it now stands, leading some governments in the area to doubt that a negotiated settlement is possible there, diplomatic sources said this week....
>
> The U.S. effort already appears to have borne fruit, as these three countries in the past week have backed off from previous, unofficial expressions of support for the treaty.[21]

The United States was successful in having the treaty rejected.

This treaty offered the United States almost everything it said it wanted: a ban on arms imports by Nicaragua, withdrawal of virtually all Cuban or Soviet military advisers, guarantees against foreign bases, and the elimination of any shipment of arms from Nicaragua to El Salvador. To verify all this, a commission was to be set up with members from agreed-upon neutral nations which would have had sweeping powers of on-site inspection in order to monitor compliance by all parties to the treaty. But these gains came at a price. The draft agreement also called for an end to military intervention by the United States, and that was not what the Reagan administration had in mind.

Another opportunity for Contadora came in 1986. This time the United States prevented agreement by threatening that it would continue the contra war (with $100 million in newly-approved funding) even after Nicaragua signed the proposed treaty. The Nicaraguan government was not willing to move toward military de-escalation under these conditions.[22]

In 1987 Costa Rican President Oscar Arias suggested an alternative approach. Meeting in Guatemala City, on August 7 the presidents of five Central American nations reached agreement on a compromise based on both Contadora and the Arias plan. This accord, known as Esquipulas II, contained some but not all of Contadora's provisions; it obligated all five governments to take steps toward reconciliation with their unarmed domestic political opposition and to restore full civil liberties, while preventing any use of their national territory for attacks on other countries or support of guerrilla movements. Other key features of the unsigned Contadora treaty, such as ending arms imports and banning foreign military advisors and exercises, were set aside for future negotiation.[23]

The initial U.S. government reaction to the peace agreement was openly negative.[24] To millions of Central Americans, however, the agreement brought renewed hope for an end to long years of suffering and civil war. World opinion was overwhelmingly supportive, highlighted on October 13 by the announcement that President Arias would receive the Nobel Peace Prize for his initiative. Washington subsequently muted its direct criticism, and sought instead to focus U.S. public attention on alleged shortcomings in Nicaragua's compliance with the accord while ignoring the extent to which other governments, especially Honduras', failed to carry out their own obligations. Most important, the Reagan administration and its political allies have worked to ensure continued U.S. military support for the contra forces, and hence for the continuation of the war in Nicaragua. If these efforts are successsful, they will undercut the peace agreement at its central point.

It is folly for the United States to oppose these promising avenues to peace. The U.S. government should encourage and support regional peace initiatives such as Contadora and Esquipulas II, both of which have included ample provisions to satisfy legitimate U.S. security concerns. In addition, the United States must be willing to negotiate any remaining problems directly with Nicaragua or other countries.

6. *The United States should seek international arrangements to relieve the economic crisis* facing Central America. These arrangements must respect the right to self-determination of the region's nations and the basic human needs of its people.

The causes of the crisis are many, including falling world prices for the region's agricultural exports, rising prices of imports including oil, rising interest rates on foreign debts, and (except for Costa Rica) the high costs of military buildups and conflicts. Genuine peace is a precondition for a solution to the crisis, and would in itself be a giant step forward. A variety of reforms, including in some countries major land reform, will also be required. The United States can not dictate, but should encourage, such changes. Ending the massive U.S. military involvement in the region would save many billions of dollars per year, and these funds could be channeled through international agencies to promote genuine development and to meet human needs.[25]

* * *

These measures are intended to reduce both the suffering now caused by small wars and the danger of creating larger ones in the future. Much of that suffering and danger has roots in past and present U.S. insistence on hegemony. Recognizing that U.S. security needs can be addressed more effectively through negotiations than by seeking military control, and that the United States has no economic or political interests in the region which it must impose at gunpoint, makes it possible to reject the "need" for domination.

Ending the U.S. military role in regional conflicts would set the stage for a new policy. Turning rhetoric into reality, the United States should resolve that peace, human rights and social justice are basic values for all people and consider how it might help its neighbors achieve these goals. It must be recognized that progress may not come easily, even with good intentions. Democracy and respect for human rights cannot be exported, least of all by military force; they can at most be encouraged when the local conditions are right.

To make these changes in U.S. policy will take courage—courage to put away exaggerated fears of revolution and of communism, and courage to accept social diversity and non-alignment. The gains for our Central American neighbors could be great, but the United States would benefit too. Current policy is a tragic failure; U.S. control has not been secured, and the moral standing and credibility of the United States have suffered badly. A new policy could repair this damage, and regain for the United States a measure of that respect and credibility due to a great nation which obeys international law, keeps its agreements, and behaves in harmony with the high ideals it proclaims.

Notes to Chapter 1

1. *Voices of Experience in Central America: Former Peace Corps Volunteers' Insights Into a Troubled Region,* Returned Peace Corps Volunteers Committee on Central America, Washington, D.C., 1985, page 38. The volunteer quoted, a university teacher who served in El Salvador in 1977 and 1978, was replying to the question "What are the most serious misconceptions you feel Americans have regarding your country of service?"

2. George Kennan, "On Nuclear War," *New York Review of Books,* January 21, 1982.

3. Stephen F. Cohen, *Sovieticus: American Perceptions and Soviet Realities* (New York: Norton, 1985), pages 19-21. This book is based on Cohen's column "Sovieticus" which appears in *The Nation* magazine. The column quoted here, "Sovietophobia—Our Other Soviet Problem," was first published on April 9, 1983.

4. *Ibid.,* pages 29-31. The original date of "The American Media and the Soviet Union" was May 12, 1984.

5. Ibid.

6. Ibid. For one example of how the original charges have fared, see "Yellow Rain Evidence Slowly Whittled Away" by Eliot Marshall, *Science,* July 4, 1986.

7. Conor Cruise O'Brien, "God and Man in Nicaragua," *The Atlantic,* August, 1986.

8. Bernard Gwertzman, "Two Hawks and a Dove: How They Look at the Indochina War Now," *New York Times,* April 30, 1985.

9. John B. Oakes, "Mr. Reagan's 'Flim-Flamming'" (Op-ed article), *New York Times,* April 17, 1985.

10. Latin American Studies Association, *The Electoral Process in Nicaragua: Domestic and International Influences,* November 19, 1984, page 32.

11. A recent study of the inadequacy of elections as sole determinant of "democracy" is Edward Herman and Frank Brodhead, *Demonstration Elections: U.S.-Staged Elections in the Dominican Republic, Vietnam, and El Salvador* (Boston: South End Press, 1984).

12. Enrique E. Rivarola, "Some Aspects of Soviet-Latin American Relations," in J. Gregory Oswald and Anthony Strover, editors, *The Soviet Union and Latin America* (New York: Praeger Publishers, 1970), page 61.

13. See, for example, Stephen B. Oates, *Let the Trumpet Sound: The Life of Martin Luther King Jr.* (New York: Harper and Row, 1982).

14. Viewing Central American issues primarily from an East/West perspective is a common feature of nearly all the U.S. government documents cited in this book. A relatively sophisticated exposition of the East/West thesis is the *Report of the National Bipartisan Commission on Central America* (the "Kissinger Commission"), submitted to the President January 10, 1984. For analysis of the *Report's* approach see William M. LeoGrande, "Through the Looking Glass: The Report of the National Bipartisan Commission on Central America," *World Policy Journal,* Winter 1984; as well as Phillip Berryman, "The Kissinger Report: A Critique," American Friends Service Committee, January 1984.

15. "Central America: Defending Our Vital Interests," address by President Reagan to Joint Session of Congress, April 27, 1983.

Notes to Chapter 2

1. A short factual account of the missile crisis is Barton Bernstein, "The Week We Almost Went To War," *Bulletin of the Atomic Scientists,* February 1976, pages 12-21. Newly released information does nothing to diminish the seriousness of the crisis; see Seymour Hersh, "Was Castro Out of Control in 1962?" *Washington Post,* October 11, 1987.

2. All the Central American nations have signed and ratified the treaty, and the current Nicaraguan government affirms its continued support. Cuba declined to sign, partly because the U.S.-controlled territories of Puerto Rico, the Virgin Islands, the Panama Canal Zone and the U.S. naval base within Cuba (Guantanamo Bay) were originally not included. The Carter administration in 1977 signed Protocol I which brought these areas under the treaty's provisions, and that action was ratified in 1981. (U.S. Arms Control and Disarmament Agency, *Arms Control and Disarmament Agreements: Texts and Histories of Negotiations,* 1982 or later edition.) Questions have recently been raised about U.S. compliance; see below and note 9. The importance of Cuba's failure to sign the treaty is limited by the Soviet acceptance of Protocol II and by the 1962 U.S-Soviet "understanding."

3. *U.S. News and World Report,* June 13, 1983, page 25.

4. These figures are from *The Military Balance 1987-1988,* published by the International Institute for Strategic Studies in London, England (autumn, 1987).

5. Joseph Cirincione and Leslie Hunter, "Military Threats, Actual and Potential," in Robert S. Leiken (editor), *Central America: Anatomy of Conflict* (New York: Pergamon Press, 1984), page 173.

6. "Campaign '84: The Inside Story," *Newsweek Election Extra,* November-December 1984, page 32.

7. The U.S. military presence in Central America and the Caribbean is outlined in the "Almanac" issue (September/October 1986) of *Defense '86,* published by the Department of Defense.

8. NARMIC interview with Lt. Col. Sontag of U.S. Atlantic Command, November 1986.

9. Report of the Puerto Rican Bar Association, August 1984, as cited in Catherine A. Sunshine, *The Caribbean: Survival, Struggle and Sovereignty* (Boston: South End Press, 1985), page 174. A fuller account of the Bar Association investigation is Judith Berkan, Charles Hey-Maestre and Pedro Saade-Llorens, "Violating the Treaty of Tlatelolco," *Arms Control Today,* January 1985, page 4. Charles

Van Doren's "U.S. In Compliance With Tlatelolco Treaty—A Rebuttal," *Arms Control Today,* February/March 1985, page 3, seems less than convincing. See also Leslie Gelb, "U.S. Has Contingency Plan to Put A-Arms in 4 Countries, Aides Say," *New York Times,* February 13, 1985. (Puerto Rico is one of the four.)

10. Many press reports and other sources describe the U.S. military buildup and activities, among them Bill Keller, "Army General Chosen as New Latin Commander," *New York Times,* January 12, 1985; Fred Hiatt, "Entrenching in Honduras," *Washington Post,* February 18, 1986; Lloyd Grove, "In Honduras, Uneasy Days and Crazy Nights," *Washington Post,* October 20, 1986; many articles in *Honduras Update* including Leyda Barbieri and Susan Jessop, "Unending Temporary Presence," November/December 1986; and *Invasion: A Guide to the U.S. Military Presence in Central America,* NARMIC/American Friends Service Committee, May 1985. See also Medea Benjamin (translator and editor), *Don't Be Afraid, Gringo* (San Francisco: Institute for Food and Development Policy, 1987), Appendix 6 (pages 162-165).

11. *White House Digest,* "The Strategic and Economic Importance of the Caribbean Sea Lanes," April 4, 1984.

12. U.S. GAO, "Assessment of Factors Affecting the Availability of U.S. Oil Supplies From the Caribbean," September 13, 1985, pages iii, 28 and 29. This report contains an amusing insight into official language. As originally written it mentioned the "U.S. invasion" of Grenada. When the draft was submitted to the Defense Department for review, the GAO was informed that "The October 1983 U.S. military action in Grenada was a rescue mission and should not be characterized as an invasion in U.S. Government publications." The GAO authors compromised on "military operation." The DoD also requested changes in the report to make it show more concern about Soviet access to the region and about threats to shipping in case of a hypothetical "general war."

13. Quoted in Raymond Bonner, *Weakness and Deceit: U.S. Policy and El Salvador* (New York: Times Books, 1984), page 235.

14. Cirincione and Hunter, *op. cit.* page 188.

15. NARMIC interview, November 1985.

16. NARMIC interview with Lt. Col. Sontag of U.S. Atlantic Command, November 1986.

17. *The Defense Monitor,* Vol. XV, number 4, 1986; *Defense '86,* "Almanac" issue, 1986. *Jane's Fighting Ships 1986-87* (London: Jane's Publishing Company) states that the Midway has been based in Yokosuka, Japan since 1973.

18. A.A. Gromyko and B.N. Ponomarev, editors, *Soviet Foreign Policy* (Moscow: Progress Publisher, 1981, English edition).

19. These figures are from the U.S. Department of State, *Soviet and East European Aid to the Third World, 1981,* February 1983, as quoted in *The Jacobsen Report: Soviet Attitudes Towards, Aid To, and Contacts With Central American Revolutionaries,* June 1984, page 16. This report was prepared for

the Department of State by Carl G. Jacobsen and colleagues at the University of Miami.

20. Jonathan Steele, *Soviet Power: The Kremlin's Foreign Policy—Brezhnev to Chernenko* (New York: Simon and Schuster, 1984), page 168.

21. Soviet diplomatic and trade relations with Latin America are described in Cole Blasier, *The Giant's Rival: The USSR and Latin America* (University of Pittsburgh Press, 1983), especially chapters 2 and 3.

22. Communist parties played major roles in organizing insurrections in El Salvador (1932), Chile (1934) and Brazil (1935). For a brief history of communism in Latin America see Marc Edelman, "The Other Super Power: The Soviet Union and Latin America, 1917-1987," *NACLA Report on the Americas,* January/February 1987, pages 10-40. The role of communist parties in Nicaragua and modern-day El Salvador will be discussed in chapters 3 and 4.

23. The figures for Italy are from *The World Factbook: 1986* published by the Central Intelligence Agency, page 124.

24. See chapters 1 and 2 of Andres Suarez, *Cuba: Castroism and Communism, 1959-1966* (Cambridge: M.I.T. Press, 1967). In his introduction to this book M.I.T. Professor Ernst Halperin states that "Dr. Suarez is not the first to point out that the old, established Communist party, the PSP, played only a minor role in the Cuban revolution. But he is the first to document this so thoroughly and extensively." See also Edelman, *op.cit.,* pages 19-21. The recent biography by journalist Tad Szulc, *Fidel: A Critical Portrait* (New York: William Morrow and Company, 1986), argues that Castro adopted Marx-ist models of social change and initiated cooperation with the "old communists" (the PSP) earlier than has generally been recognized. Whether or not this view is accurate, it remains true that the PSP was not a major actor in the overthrow of the Batista regime.

25. See Carla Anne Robbins, *The Cuban Threat* (Philadelphia: ISHI Publications, 1985), page 17; also Edelman, *op.cit.,* pages 20-21. Much of the following account of Cuban foreign policy is based on *The Cuban Threat.*

26. Quoted in Suarez, *op. cit.,* page 175.   ·

27. Robbins, *op. cit.,* pages 42-44.

28. In 1971 the Defense Intelligence Agency estimated during congressional testimony that between 2150 and 2500 Latin Americans received "subversive training" in Cuba during the 1960s; the training was not always military. (Cited in Robbins, *Cuban Threat,* page 53.) Earlier U.S. government estimates ranged from 10,000 to 25,000.

29. These figures are from U.S. government agencies; see Department of Defense, *Military Assistance and Foreign Military Sales Facts,* March 1971, as well as Michael T. Klare and Cynthia Arnson, *Supplying Repression: U.S. Support for Authoritarian Regimes Abroad* (Washington: The Institute for Policy Studies, 1981), pages 20 and 48.

30. Cuba's thwarted rapprochment with the United States and involvements in Angola and Ethiopia are described more fully in Robbins, *Cuban Threat,* pages 192-237.

31. John Stockwell, *In Search of Enemies: A CIA Story* (New York: W.W. Norton, 1978), page 43.

32. For the administration's conception of Cuba's role, see U.S. Departments of State and Defense, *The Soviet-Cuban Connection in Central America and the Caribbean,* March 1985.

Notes to Chapter 3

1. Address to the Baltimore Council on Foreign Affairs, September 12, 1983.

2. General Smedley D. Butler, "America's Armed Forces," *Common Sense,* October 1935 through February 1936 (an article in five parts). These quotations are from part one, page 6 and part two (November), page 8 respectively.

3. Butler describes the Nicaragua intervention in part 3, December 1935, pages 13-14.

4. President Reagan used these words as he declared the national emergency and the embargo on May 1, 1985; see *New York Times,* May 2, 1985, page 8.

5. Jacobsen report, page 6. (See note 19, chapter 2.)

6. See Robert Armstrong, Marc Edelman, and Robert Matthews, "Sandinista Foreign Policy: Strategies for Survival", *NACLA Report on the Americas,* May/June 1985, page 36.

7. For the Carter administration's policy, see William LeoGrande, "The United States and the Nicaraguan Revolution," chapter 3 in Thomas W. Walker (editor), *Nicaragua in Revolution* (New York: Praeger Publishers, 1982).

8. Howard Wiarda and Harvey Kline (editors), *Latin American Politics and Development* (Boulder, CO: Westview Press, 1985), chapter 21, especially page 509.

9. Walker, op cit, pages 73-75.

10. Armstrong, *et. al., op. cit.,* especially pages 31, 32 and 38.

11. Jacobsen report, page 21.

12. Armstrong, *et. al., op. cit.,* page 32.

13. U.S. Departments of State and Defense, *The Challenge to Democracy in Central America,* October 1986.

14. The administration's "internal" charges against the Sandinistas shift ground frequently and touch nearly all aspects of society; thus a point-by-point analysis is difficult and can never answer all the accusations. The most satisfactory response is a general study of the Nicaraguan revolution. Many useful accounts are available. One example is Thomas W. Walker (editor), *Nicaragua: The First Five Years* (New York: Praeger Publishers, 1985).

15. Ibid, chapters 6 and 14-16.

16. *Americas Watch Report on Human Rights in Nicaragua,* July 1985, page 3. A comparative study of Central American records on human rights can be found

in the more comprehensive Americas Watch report *With Friends Like These* edited by Cynthia Brown (New York: Pantheon Books, 1985), chapter 4. Since those reports were written the situation in Guatemala has changed; the first civilian government in many years took office early in 1986 and the violations of human rights are now less open and less extreme. Yet political murders continued during 1986 along with severe repression of the rural Indian population, no investigations or trials for past offenses have taken place, and Guatemala's president acknowledges that he must compete with the armed forces leadership for a share of power to govern. (See Allan Nairn and Jean-Marie Simon, "Bureaucracy of Death," *New Republic,* June 30, 1986.) In Nicaragua the government has acknowledged its past mistakes in dealing with the Miskito population and embarked on a process of reconciliation and establishment of limited autonomy for the Indian peoples of the East coast.

17. Latin American Studies Association, *The Electoral Process in Nicaragua: Domestic and International Influences,* November 1984. The quoted passages are from the Summary of Findings preceding page 1.

18. For a description see Andrew Reding, "Nicaragua's New Constitution," *World Policy Journal,* Spring, 1987.

19. See, for example, *Human Rights in Nicaragua, 1986: An Americas Watch Report,* February 1987, chapter II. More references to the consequences of the war will be found in chapter 5.

20. Departments of State and Defense, *The Sandinista Military Build-up,* May 1985. The passages quoted are on pages 36 and 39 respectively.

21. Departments of State and Defense, *The Soviet-Cuban Connection in Central America and the Caribbean,* March 1985, page 28.

22. State Department and Pentagon *Congressional Presentation Document,* Security Assistance Programs, FY 1981, quoted in "Sandinista Foreign Policy," page 24.

23. Humberto Ortega, "El Carácter Defensivo del Ejército Popular Sandinista," *Barricada* (Managua), April 13, 1985.

24. Clifford Krauss and Robert Greenberger, "Despite Fears of U.S., Soviet Aid to Nicaragua Appears to Be Limited," *Wall Street Journal,* April 3, 1985.

25. For the Soviet statements see the Jacobsen report, pages 5 and 12.

26. See Dennis Gilbert, "Nicaragua," chapter 4 in Morris Blachman, William Leogrande and Kenneth Sharpe (editors), *Confronting Revolution: Security Through Diplomacy in Central America* (New York: Pantheon Books, 1986), pages 118-124; see also William M. LeoGrande, "The United States and Nicaragua," chapter 21 in Walker (editor), *Nicaragua: The First Five Years, op. cit.,* especially pages 437-439 and 442-444. Accounts of specific instances include Patrick Tyler, "Sandinistas Propose 4 Security Accords to U.S.," *Washington Post,* October 21, 1983 and Gerald Boyd, "White House Scorns Peace Offer From Nicaragua," *New York Times,* March 1, 1985. Nicaragua's position toward the Contadora process is discussed in chapter 5 below.

27. These are U.S. government figures from *The Challenge To Democracy in Central America*, pages 22-23.

28. *The Sandinista Military Build-up, op. cit.*, pages 7 and 11. In November 1986 *The Challenge to Democracy* stated that "The Sandinista armored force today totals about 350 tanks and armored vehicles" (page 20), implying little or no growth since the publication of *Build-up* in May 1985; *Challenge* gives no corresponding figures for artillery. *The Military Balance 1986-87* published by the International Institute for Strategic Studies (IISS) in London confirmed the no-growth figure of 110 T-54/55 tanks, but the 1987-1988 edition states that 40 more of these tanks have arrived. Both editions credit Nicaragua with 30 122 mm and 36 152 mm howitzers, a modest increase since early 1985.

At times the U.S. government's figures for Nicaraguan weaponry have exceeded estimates from other analysts by as much as a factor of two. A "CDI Fact Sheet" from the Center for Defense Information issued in February 1985 compares differing figures from several sources; for example, the IISS in the fall of 1984 said Nicaragua had 60 T-54 and T-55 tanks, while in July 1984 the State Department stated that it had 100 such tanks. A comparative summary entitled "The Military Balance in Central America: An Analysis and Critical Evaluation of Administration Claims" was published in April 1985 by the Council on Hemispheric Affairs.

In general, these differences are not critical to assessments of Nicaragua's military potential. In some instances specific errors in the government's figures have been documented. Here is an example, quoted from the Jacobsen report, page 17:

> The US administration asserts that Cuba has built and is building a total of 36 new military bases in Nicaragua. One of the sites mentioned, Tipitapa, has been visited by a number of Western journalists; the construction in question is that of a very large sugar plant—among the workers are 100 Cuban technicians.

29. Edward King, *Out of Step, Out of Line: U.S. Military Policy in Central America,* Unitarian Universalist Service Committee, September 1984, pages 24 and 25.

30. Edward King, *The Nicaraguan Armed Forces: A Second Look,* Unitarian Universalist Service Committee, April 1985, page 13.

31. *Honduras and U.S. Policy: An Enduring Dilemma,* Hearing before the Subcommittee on Inter-American Affairs of the Committee on Foreign Affairs, U.S. House of Representatives, September 21, 1982. The quotation from Col. Buchanan's testimony is on page 52.

32. NARMIC interview, November 1986.

33. Krauss and Greenberger, "Soviet Aid to Nicaragua."

34. The numbers of fixed-wing aircraft are from *The Military Balance 1987-1988,* which adds that "Most of the fixed-wing combat aircraft inventory, however, is thought to be nonoperational" (page 177). The same source reports that Nicaragua has 34 Mi-8/-17 and 12 Mi-24/-25 helicopters, in good agree-

ment with the estimate of "10 to 15" Mi-24/-25s from Stephen Kinzer, "Nicaragua Assails U.S. Plan on Jets," *New York Times,* October 31, 1986, as well as with an estimate of "over a dozen" from Col. John Buchanan in November 1986 (NARMIC interview). The *Military Balance* figures also agree with the reported total of "40 to 50" helicopters in Kinzer, "Nicaragua Said to Seek More Soviet Helicopters," *New York Times,* April 7, 1987, where it is attributed to "military and diplomatic sources in Managua."

35. Edward King, *op. cit.,* page 21.

36. Bernard Gwertzman, "U.S. Set To Offer Newer Jet Fighter To the Hondurans," and Kinzer, "Nicaragua Assails U.S. Plan on Jets," both in *New York Times,* October 31, 1986.

37. Larry Rohter, "Nicaragua Says It Will Suspend Arms Buildup," *New York Times,* February 28, 1985. Nicaragua's unilateral moratorium on advanced aircraft was grudgingly acknowledged by the U.S. State Department in Special Report No. 124, "Sustaining a Consistent Policy in Central America: One Year After the National Bipartisan Commission Report," April 1985, page 14. This report describes Nicaragua's move as "designed primarily for public-relations impact," and adds that it is "potentially significant, but only if it proves more far-reaching and permanent." This luke-warm response to Nicaragua's moratorium is in contrast to the excited rhetoric and threats with which the Reagan administration greeted (false) reports that MIG fighter aircraft were en route to Nicaragua in November 1984. As of autumn, 1987, the moratorium is apparently still in effect despite the U.S./Honduran escalation.

38. For Nicaragua's offer to negotiate, see *New York Times,* May 28, 1986, page 3. Concerning the modern jets for Honduras, see the two *New York Times* articles cited in note 36, plus Elaine Sciolino, "White House to Push Sale of Jets to Honduras," *New York Times,* May 12, 1987.

39. *The Sandinista Military Build-up, op. cit.* pages 20 and 40.

40. Edward King, *op. cit.,* page 5.

41. *The Sandinista Military Build-up, op. cit.* page 36.

42. Armstrong, *et. al.,* page 24.

43. George Black and Robert Matthews, "Arms From the USSR—Or From Nobody," *The Nation,* August 31, 1985, page 148. The figures of $12 million for Soviet military aid during 1979 and 1980 and $45 million in 1981 are in the 1984 "classified U.S.intelligence report" described by the *Wall Street Journal;* see note 24.

44. The Nicaraguan search for military aid is described in Armstrong, *et. al., op. cit.,* and by Black and Matthews in "Arms From the USSR," cited above.

45. For the numbers of students at the School of the Americas see *Army,* January 1983, page 27, or the school's annual *Fact Book.* The training of Nicaraguans ended in 1978, but El Salvador and Honduras have sent many students during the 1980s. The quotation is from the *Miami Herald,* February 2, 1981, cited by Armstrong, *et. al., op. cit.,* page 26.

46. The Neutrality Act (18 U.S.C. 960) makes it a crime to initiate or organize on U.S. territory a hostile military expedition against a country with which the United States is not at war. A strong case can be made that the actions of U.S. government officials and their supporters in arming the contras violate this law. See for example *Memorandum of the National Emergency Civil Liberties Committee on the United States, Nicaragua and the World Court,* published by the Committee in New York, April 1985.

47. Israel's role in Central America goes beyond aiding the Guatemalan government; it was a major, and ultimately the only, supplier of arms to Somoza's National Guard in Nicaragua and has also sent weapons to the contra forces. For more information and documentation see Haifa University Professor Benjamin Beit-Hallahmi's article "U.S.-Israeli-Central America Connection" in *The Link,* published by Americans for Middle East Understanding, November 1985, pages 1-13, or chapter four in the same author's *The Israeli Connection: Who Israel Arms and Why* (New York: Pantheon Books, 1987).

48. *Sandinista Foreign Policy,* page 30.

49. Jacobsen report, page 19.

50. Walker (editor), *op. cit.,* page 24.

Notes to Chapter 4

1. Departments of State and Defense, *The Soviet-Cuban Connection in Central America and the Caribbean*, March 1985, page 31.

2. "Storm Over El Salvador," *Newsweek*, March 16, 1981, pages 34-39.

3. Duarte is quoted by Raymond Bonner in the *New York Times Magazine*, February 22, 1981. An overlapping quote is found in Bonner's book *Weakness and Deceit: U.S. Policy and El Salvador* (New York: Times Books, 1984), page 24.

4. The most complete account of the 1932 rebellion, which includes these estimates, is Thomas P. Anderson, *Matanza: El Salvador's Communist Revolt of 1932* (Lincoln: University of Nebraska Press, 1971).

5. Bonner, *Weakness and Deceit, op. cit.,* page 30. It is likely that at least one of the junta members was indeed sympathetic to the Cuban revolution.

6. Tommy Sue Montgomery, *Revolution in El Salvador: Origins and Evolution* (Boulder, CO: Westview Press, 1982), page 73.

7. Bonner, *Weakness and Deceit, op. cit.,* page 30. (This remark by John Kennedy has been widely quoted, and can also be found in *Matanza.*)

8. José Napoleón Duarte (with Diana Page), *Duarte: My Story* (New York: G.P.Putnam's Sons, 1986), page 91. See also Bonner, *Weakness and Deceit,* pages 32-33.

9. Duarte, *op. cit.,* page 95; Bonner, *Weakness and Deceit, op. cit.,* pages 34-35.

10. Penny Lernoux, *Cry of the People* (New York: Penguin Books, 1982), page 37.

11. Montgomery, *Revolution in El Salvador,* pages 97-98.

12. Ibid., page 18. On page 198 Montgomery cites the Commission on Human Rights of El Salvador as reporting 105 people killed by security forces and the right-wing vigilante organization ORDEN between October 15 and November 3, while the figure for the whole of 1979 up to October 15 was 475. More generally, Montgomery says that "according to both human rights and church organizations, 80 percent of the more than 10,000 deaths in the country during 1980 were caused by government forces, ORDEN, or right-wing death squads."

13. Ibid., pages 19-20; Bonner, *Weakness and Deceit, op. cit.,* pages 164-167.

14. Bonner, *Weakness and Deceit, op. cit.,* pages 172-173.

15. See Americas Watch Committee and the American Civil Liberties Union, *Report on Human Rights in El Salvador* (New York: Vintage Books, 1982), pages vii and 278-281; or Richard Alan White, *The Morass: United States Intervention in Central America* (New York: Harper and Row, 1984), pages 43-49. Data on the number of murders were compiled by the legal aid office of the Archdiocese of San Salvador.

16. Thomas P. Anderson, "El Salvador," chapter 4 in Robert Wesson (editor), *Communism in Central America and the Caribbean* (Stanford, CA: Hoover Institution Press, 1982), page 70.

17. *Newsweek*, "Storm Over El Salvador." *op. cit.*

18. Ray Bonner, *Weakness and Deceit, op. cit.*, pages 90-91. Chapter 6 of this book gives a useful short history of the Salvadoran left.

19. Ronald Reagan, "Strategic Importance of El Salvador and Central America," speech to National Association of Manufacturers, March 10, 1983; published by the Department of State as Current Policy No. 464.

20. This account of the "invasion" is based on Bonner, *Weakness and Deceit, op. cit.*, pages 225-227.

21. U.S. Department of State, Special Report No. 80: *Communist Interference in El Salvador,* February 23, 1981.

22. Phillip Berryman, "The State Department White Paper 'Communist Interference in El Salvador,'" AFSC memorandum, March 3, 1981; James Petras, "White Paper on the White Paper," *The Nation,* March 28, 1981.

23. Jonathan Kwitney, "Apparent Errors Cloud U.S. 'White Paper' on Reds in El Salvador," *Wall Street Journal,* June 8, 1981; Robert Kaiser, "Flaws in El Salvador White Paper Raise Questions About its Analysis," *The Washington Post,* June 9, 1981.

24. Dr. Clements's experience is described in his book *Witness to War: An American Doctor in El Salvador* (New York: Bantam Books, 1984); the quotation is from page 83. A 30-minute film (also entitled "Witness to War") about Dr. Clements and his work in El Salvador, produced by David Goodman, won the 1985 Academy Award for "best short documentary."

25. Ibid, page 53.

26. Ibid, page 123.

27. Bonner, *Weakness and Deceit, op. cit.*, pages 117-132 and 266-269.

28. Leslie H. Gelb, "U.S. Aides See Need for Big Effort To Avert Rebel Victory in Salvador," *New York Times,* April 22, 1983. The article reports interviews with "more than a score" of administration officials. While these officials insisted on the importance of Cuban and Nicaraguan support for the rebels, they also "acknowledge that the guerrillas are now getting most of their arms from within El Salvador, by capturing or buying them."

29. Edward King, *The Nicaraguan Armed Forces, op. cit.*, page 23. (See note 30, chapter 3.)

30. Departments of State and Defense, *Background Paper: Central America*, May 27, 1983; *Background Paper: Nicaragua's Military Build-up and Support For Central American Subversion*, July 18, 1984.

31. *Background Paper: Nicaragua's Military Build-up, op. cit.*, page 19.

32. King, *The Nicaraguan Armed Forces*, page 24.

33. Departments of State and Defense, *News Briefing on Intelligence Information on External Support of the Guerrillas in El Salvador*, August 8, 1984.

34. NARMIC interview in November 1985; see below and note 36.

35. King, *The Nicaraguan Armed Forces, op. cit.*, page 26.

36. MacMichael's qualifications include a PhD in history, ten years in the U.S. Marine Corps, and twelve years working at Stanford Research Institute studying insurgent movements in the Third World. At the time of the interview he was a research associate at the Council on Hemispheric Affairs in Washington, D.C.

37. "US Halts Economic Aid to Nicaragua," *New York Times*, April 2, 1981.

38. The article "US Backed Rebel Army Swells to 7000 Men" by Don Oberdorfer and Patrick E. Tyler, *Washington Post*, May 8, 1983 describes the March 9, 1981 "Presidential Finding" endorsing covert action against Nicaragua.

39. U.S. Department of State, *"Revolution Beyond Our Borders": Sandinista Intervention in Central America*, September 1985.

40. Ibid. The title of this paper is taken from a July 19, 1981 speech by Comandante Tomás Borge, who is quoted out of context. Here is the quote as given by the State Department:

> This revolution goes beyond our borders. Our revolution was always internationalist from the moment Sandino fought [his first battle].

And for comparison here is a longer excerpt from the same speech with the State Department's quotation in italics:

> Nicaragua is no longer unknown. Now it is part of the wave of revolutions in our era. It is a country with great moral authority, not only in Central America, not only in Latin America, but in the whole world. We are proud to be Nicaraguans. *This revolution transcends national boundaries.*
>
> *Our revolution has always been internationalist, ever since Sandino fought* in the Segovias. There were internationalists from all over the world who fought alongside Sandino, men from Venezuela, Mexico, Peru. Another who fought alongside Sandino was the great hero of the Salvadoran people named Farabundo Martí.
>
> It is not strange that we are internationalists, because this is something we got from Sandino. All the revolutionaries and all the

peoples of Latin America especially know that our people's heart
is with them, beats alongside theirs....This does not mean that we
export our revolution. It is enough—and we couldn't do otherwise—for us to export our example, the example of the courage,
sensitivity and determination of our people.

How could we not be upset about the injustices that are
committed in different parts of the world? But we know that it is
the people themselves of these countries who must make their
revolutions, and we know that by advancing our revolution we
are also helping our brothers and sisters in the rest of Latin
America....Our internationalism is primarily expressed by con-
solidating our own revolution, working selflessly day in and day
out and training ourselves militarily to defend our homeland.

The fuller quotation from Borge's speech is from Bruce Marcus (editor), *Sandinistas Speak: Speeches, Writings and Interviews With Leaders of Nicaragua's
Revolution* (New York: Pathfinder Press, 1982), page 132. The State
Department's out-of-context excerpt was used earlier in the same deceptive
way by Deputy Assistant Secretary of Defense Nestor Sanchez in his article
"Revolutionary Change and the Nicaraguan People," *Strategic Review,* Summer
1984, page 18.

41. *"Jane's "* refers to *Jane's Weapon Systems 1986-1987* (London: Jane's
Publishing Co., 1987, and earlier editions), a standard reference on military
technology.

42. A brief account is Paul Lewis, "World Court Supports Nicaragua After U.S.
Rejected Judges' Role," *New York Times,* June 28, 1986. A more complete
analysis, including the excerpts quoted here, is "World Court Rules That U.S.
Policy Toward Nicaragua Violates International Law," *Update,* Central American
Historical Institute, Washington, D.C., July 23, 1986.

Notes to Chapter 5

1. This statement was made during an April 14, 1984 radio broadcast, and is quoted in the State and Defense Departments' 1984 *Background Paper: Nicaragua's Military Build-up and Support for Central American Subversion,* page 2.

2. President Reagan, "Central America: Defending Our Vital Interests," address to a joint session of Congress, April 27, 1983. (U.S. Department of State, Current Policy No. 482.)

3. The remark about "100 million people" was made in a television address on May 9, 1984 and is quoted here from *The Soviet-Cuban Connection,* page 2.

4. Frank A. Barnett, et. al., (editors), *Special Operations in U.S. Strategy* (Washington, D.C.: National Defense University Press, 1984), page 223. (Quoted in *NACLA Report on the Americas,* April-May 1986, page 40.)

5. Secretary of State George Shultz, "Comprehensive Strategy for Central America," testimony before the Senate Foreign Relations Committee on August 4, 1983. (U.S. Department of State, Current Policy No. 502.)

6. A comprehensive review is Thomas W. Walker (editor), *Reagan versus the Sandinistas: The Undeclared War on Nicaragua* (Boulder and London: Westview Press, 1987).

7. For the contras' history and human rights practices, see Christopher Dickey, *With the Contras: A Reporter in the Wilds of Nicaragua* (New York: Simon and Schuster, 1985). A study enumerating the former Somoza Guardsmen among their leaders is "Who Are the Contras?" prepared by the staff of the Arms Control and Foreign Policy Caucus of the U.S. Congress, *Congressional Record,* April 23, 1985, pages H2335-H2339. The Americas Watch quote is from Brown, *With Friends Like These,* page 175. (See chapter 3, note 16.) See also Reed Brody, *Contra Terror in Nicaragua: Report of a Fact-Finding Mission, September 1984-January 1985* (Boston: South End Press, 1985), as well as *Human Rights in Nicaragua, 1986* (chapter 3, note 19). Efforts to improve the contras' image have not been successful; see Russell Watson *et al,* "The Contras Won't Change," *Newsweek,* April 13, 1987, and Rod Nordland, "The New Contras?" *Newsweek,* June 1, 1987.

8. U.S. Department of State, *Patterns of Global Terrorism: 1983,* September 1984.

9. See William LeoGrande, *Central America and the Polls,* Washington Office on Latin America Special Report, May 1984, for an analysis covering the early

1980s; there is a 1987 update. For 1986 poll results, see the *New York Times,* June 5, 1986.

10. Louis Wiznitzer, "U.S. Standing in Latin America Plummets," *Christian Science Monitor,* April 14, 1985; Daniel Siegel, Tom Spaulding and Peter Kornbluth, *Outcast Among Allies: The International Costs of Reagan's War Against Nicaragua,* Institute for Policy Studies paper, 1985.

11. Senator Patrick Leahy, "Update: Senate Nicaragua Vote," report to constituents, March 31, 1986.

12. See articles on Honduras cited in note 10, chapter 2, as well as Eva Gold, "Military Encirclement," chapter 3 in Walker (editor), *Reagan versus The Sandinistas.*

13. The administration frequently claims that its aid to Central America is mostly economic rather than mostly military. (For example, *The Soviet-Cuban Connection* makes this assertion on page 40.) This claim has been challenged by several members of Congress, who report that the administration's accounting "is flawed because it describes aid simply by which U.S. agency administers it—rather than what the aid is actually used for." The study concludes that, rather than the "three-to-one" margin of economic over military aid claimed by the administration, the truth is nearer the reverse—approximately a three-to-one ratio of military over economic assistance. "U.S. Aid to El Salvador: An Evaluation of the Past, A Proposal for the Future," by Senator Mark Hatfield and Representatives Jim Leach and George Miller, can be found in the *Congressional Record,* February 23, 1985, pages S1928-S1939; it was briefly described in the *Washington Post* on February 12, 1985. The report specifically deals with aid to El Salvador, but similar conclusions hold for Honduras. Another recent study further clarifies the aid picture; see *Help or Hindrance? United States Economic Aid in Central America,* Institute for Food and Development Policy, 1987.

The United States spends a great deal of money in Central America which is not officially called "aid" at all—for stationing U.S. troops in the region, for military construction, for nearly continuous maneuvers, and for its air and naval presence. An attempt to estimate what all this costs is Joshua Cohen and Joel Rogers, *Inequity and Intervention: The Federal Budget and Central America* (Boston: South End Press, 1986). With these (military) costs included, it is clear that humanitarian and development assistance make up a very small fraction of U.S. expenditures in the region.

14. Richard J. Hiller, Esq., "Contra Human Rights Abuses Against Honduran Civilians," a report written for the Washington Office on Latin America, *Honduras Update,* May 1986; also see Linda Drucker, "A Contra's Story," *The Progressive,* August 1986.

15. *Latin America Weekly Report,* May 30, 1986, page 5.

16. The Honduran Committee for the Defense of Human Rights (CODEH), 30-minute videotape, 1984. (Available for viewing from the American Friends Service Committee.)

17. Phillip Berryman, *Inside Central America* (New York: Pantheon Books, 1985), page 61.

18. The Olds's Memorandum is quoted in Karl Berman, *Under the Big Stick: Nicaragua and the United States Since 1848* (Boston: South End Press, 1986), page 293. Berman's Chapter 13 gives other useful background on the recent history of U.S.-Nicaragua relations.

19. Many authors have made broadly similar suggestions for a revision of U.S. policy. For examples see Berryman, *Inside Central America*, and the final three chapters in Blachman, LeoGrande and Sharpe, *Confronting Revolution* (note 26, chapter 3), where a proposed new policy is discussed in more detail than is possible here. See also *Breaking With a Bitter Past: Toward a New U.S. Relationship with Central America*, American Friends Service Committee, August 1987.

20. Philip Taubman, "U.S. Reported to Fear Sandinista Publicity Coup," *New York Times*, September 24, 1984.

21. Robert J. McCartney, "U.S. Urges Allies to Reject Contadora Plan," *Washington Post*, September 30, 1984.

22. For the government's description of events, see U.S. Department of State, *Resource Book: The Contadora Process*, published in January 1985 and subsequently updated. A brief account is *Challenge to Democracy*, page 67, which does not mention that Nicaragua agreed to sign the proposed treaty in 1984 while the U.S. allies in Central America bowed to U.S. wishes and refused. For an independent analysis of the treaty negotiations, see three reports from the Center for International Policy: Jim Morrell, *Contadora: The Treaty on Balance*, June 1985; Jim Morrell and William Goodfellow, *Contadora: Under the Gun*, May 1986; and Jim Morell, *Contadora Eludes U.S.*, January/February 1987.

23. For the text of the agreement, see *New York Times*, August 12, 1987. An interview with Panamanian economist Xabier Gorostiago offers a Central American perspective; see *NACLA Report on The Americas*, July/August 1987, pages 6-10.

24. See, for example, Neil A. Lewis, "U.S. Envoys Told to Convey Doubt Over Latin Plan," *New York Times*, August 18, 1987.

25. A brief introduction to this complex question is Richard S. Newfarmer, "The Economics of Strife," chapter 8 in *Confronting Revolution*. See also The Debt Crisis Network, *From Debt to Development: Alternatives to the International Debt Crisis* (Washington: Institute for Policy Studies, 1985).

Index

American Friends Service Committee Offices

AFSC National Office
1501 Cherry Street
Philadelphia, PA 19102

NARMIC/AFSC
1501 Cherry Street
Philadelphia, PA 19102

Southeastern Regional Office
92 Piedmont Ave NE
Atlanta, GA 30303

Middle Atlantic Regional Office
317 East 25th Street
Baltimore, MD 21218

New England Regional Office
2161 Massachusetts Ave
Cambridge, MA 02140

Great Lakes Regional Office
59 East Van Buren Suite 1400
Chicago, IL 60605

New York Metropolitan Office
15 Rutherford Place
New York, NY 10003

North Central Regional Office
4211 Grand Ave
Des Moines, IA 50312

Pacific Southwest Regional Office
980 North Fair Oaks Ave
Pasadena, CA 91103

Northern California Regional Office
2160 Lake Street
San Francisco, CA 94121

Pacific Northwest Regional Office
814 NE 40th Street
Seattle, WA 98105

Texas, Arkansas, Oaklahoma
Regional Office
1022 West 6th Street
Austin, TX 78703

Washington Office
1822 R Street NW
Washington, D.C. 20009